THE GREEN TEEN COOKBOOK

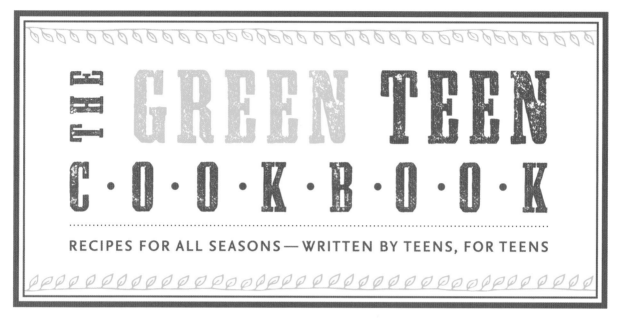

THE GREEN TEEN COOKBOOK

RECIPES FOR ALL SEASONS — WRITTEN BY TEENS, FOR TEENS

Edited by Laurane Marchive & Pam McElroy

35 Stillman Street, Suite 121
San Francisco, CA 94107
www.zestbooks.net

First published in the United States in 2014 by Zest Books
Published by arrangement with Rights People, London
Originally published in the UK as *The Green Teen Cookbook*, ed. Laurane Marchive
Copyright © 2012 Aurora Metro Publications, www.aurorametro.com
Photographs copyright © 2012 Sarah Eisenfisz, except as noted.
Photographs copyright © 2013 Zest Books: Jo Beaton: 81; Francesca Eccles: 56; Dana
  McElroy: 144 (bottom); Pam McElroy: 50, 66, 84, 108, 126, 128; Naomi Miner: 58; Tanya
  Napier: 13, 26; Serge Vejvoda: 104 (top), 122, 123
Photographs copyright © iStock: 30, 31, 32, 34, 35, 45, 93
Photographs copyright © 2013 Jan Hughes: back cover, 9, 10, 16, 18, 20, 21, 22, 23, 24, 25,
  39, 46, 48, 49, 63, 70, 71, 82, 83, 94, 98, 104, 106, 107, 116, 117, 124, 125, 127, 130, 131, 132,
  133, 142

Young Adult Nonfiction / Cooking & Food
Library of Congress control number: 2013951195
ISBN: 978-1-936976-58-4

Cover and interior design: Dagmar Trojanek and Tanya Napier

Manufactured in China
SCP 10 9 8 7 6 5 4 3 2 1
4500467143

CONNECT WITH ZEST!

zestbooks.net/blog
zestbooks.net/contests
twitter.com/zestbooks
facebook.com/zestbook
facebook.com/BooksWithATwist
pinterest.com/zestbooks

This book is dedicated to all the teens who donated recipes, cooked their own food, and allowed us to share their ideas with the world.

TABLE of CONTENTS

INTRODUCTION

As a student, I always found it hard to cook cheap, healthy food on a day-to-day basis. My refrigerator was permanently empty, and I could never be bothered to shop in the evening to pick up ingredients so I could cook something fancy. I have to confess that for a long time, I only ate pasta with store-bought tomato sauce. No oil, no butter. Maybe some salt. And it didn't taste good at all. So when I discovered (through different people, books, and websites) that it was possible to cook good food without spending a ton of time or money on it, I was more than a little surprised. Eating well didn't cost more than eating junk; in fact, it often cost a lot less.

I'm still not very far removed from my teenage years, and I know that many people, like me, don't really know how to cook healthfully and on a budget. Until recently, I didn't know what "eating ethically" meant either. So when I got the opportunity to put this cookbook together, I decided to find out.

Young people sent me recipes from all over the place, covering a wide range of different tastes and flavors. It was amazing how interested people were in the project. I asked teenagers to send me seasonal, healthful, and affordable recipes. I also asked them to send articles about food and their own experiences. And it worked!

The recipes in this book come from real teens who know what it's like to cook with little or no money. Some recipes are more or less expensive than others, some are fantastically healthy, and some a little less so. But I think variety is important—and we all need to treat ourselves every now and again, right?

I hope this cookbook helps you learn more about food, and I hope you enjoy the recipes.

—Laurane Marchive, editor

HOW TO USE THIS BOOK

When it comes to food, going green really isn't that hard to do. The recipe has been pretty much the same since the early days of the Industrial Revolution: It's still all about knowing what's in season (so that your food isn't flying halfway around the world before it winds up on your plate), finding a solid local market (so that you can purchase quality ingredients no matter what the season may be), and combining your ingredients into dishes that you'll enjoy. Technology has changed a lot of things, but when it comes to food, if you can shop seasonally, buy locally, and cook well, you've pretty much got it figured out. And if you can't, this book can help.

But before we talk more specifically about how *The Green Teen Cookbook* can help you become a healthier, more eco-conscious person, it's worth taking a step back to talk about ethical eating. Our eating habits form such an important part of our daily lives that questions of what we eat are transformed into questions of who we are. We don't say, "I eat a vegetarian diet." We say, "I am a vegetarian." Chapter 1 presents six different essays considering what our dietary choices mean and why me might make them. So whether you're a committed vegan or are just considering ways you might possibly eat a little more consciously, this is a great place to start.

The rest of the cookbook contains, as you might expect, a whole lot of recipes. Chapter 2 contains recipes for easy-to-make kitchen basics like dressings, salsas, sauces, and stock, and the rest of the book is broken down by meal type (including, of course, snacks and desserts). Every recipe in this book also has seasonal icons that let you know when the ingredients involved are in season (helping to ensure that you pay less for fresher food), and many of the recipes include bonus tips as well. Each chapter concludes with variations on classic meals—like sandwiches, salads, lasagnas, and pies—so that, no matter what the time of day or the time of year, you can always find a rock-solid option.

With the exception of the kitchen staples section and the variations on classical meals (which were written by the editors), all of the recipes in this book were submitted by teenagers. They come from all over the globe and span a huge array of culinary traditions. These recipes have all been tried and tested, but as they appear here, they also include an abundance of tips that offer possible shortcuts, cost-cuts, and recipe tweaks. Creativity is encouraged! So take what you like and adapt what you think could be better. And feel free to let us know about possible improvements. Who knows: Maybe you'll have a byline in the sequel!

However out of place you may feel in a produce market or in the kitchen, *The Green Teen Cookbook* has all the information you need to shop smarter, cook better, and eat healthier food—even on a budget. Oh, and if you forget (or never knew) how many ounces are in a cup, there's a handy table of equivalents at the back.

And with that, all of your excuses should be vanquished. So put away your embarrassment, pick a recipe, and get to green teen cooking!

—Pam McElroy, editor

A NOTE ABOUT KITCHEN SAFETY

1. Keep all knives sharp. If a knife is blunt, you have to add more pressure to cut. This means the knife becomes unstable and is more likely to bounce off of what you are cutting and into your thumb. Buy some good knives and look after them. The joy of cooking lies in using good-quality produce and equipment to channel your inventiveness.

2. Whenever possible, try using different colored chopping boards for different produce to avoid cross contamination: red boards for raw meat, blue for fish, and green or brown for fruit and vegetables. These can be picked up quite cheaply from any good cookware store. If you have a wooden chopping board, wash it, dry it, and then scrub it with a scouring pad and some fine table salt. This kills the bacteria in the nooks and crannies of the board and helps eliminate smells.

3. Lastly, be cautious: Ovens are hot, pans are heavy, and knives are sharp. Never cook when you don't feel up to it, and when it comes to food, there is an old mantra in the chef world: *If in doubt, throw it out.* Cooking should be enjoyable, so use these recipes as a reference point and don't be afraid to try something different.

Happy Cooking!!

Paul Hannagen is a young, classically French trained chef who has worked in some of the most prestigious restaurants in London. His private dining company, Cuisson, offers private dining and wine events.

A ROUGH GUIDE TO
HEALTHY, ENVIRONMENTALLY CONSCIOUS COOKING

HOW TO EAT HEALTHFULLY

BY SARAH VENIARD

Achieving balance within our mind, body, and spirit is a challenge that can sometimes seem overwhelming. With so many choices about which form of exercise we should be practicing and which foods we should (or should not) be eating, we can find ourselves going into system overload. The important thing to remember is that we are all unique. Each and every one of us is tuned differently, with varying needs and desires, and different metabolisms, and we need to find our own path to an all-around sense of well being.

Following a healthy, balanced diet may seem like a challenge if you don't know where to begin. All through your life, your body goes through changes, especially when you are evolving from an adolescent into an adult. So it's important to take good care of yourself, and the first step toward achieving this is to have a healthy diet.

Whatever diet you have chosen to follow—whether you have a no-holds barred philosophy or have chosen a vegetarian, vegan, or any other special diet—it is essential for you to get all of your nutrients in the most balanced way possible. Failing to eat a balanced diet will have negative effects on your immune system and energy levels. If you get it right, however, you can be at the peak of health. And it's actually pretty easy to cover all of the important food groups—even on a budget.

VITAMINS AND MINERALS

To begin with, it's vital that you have enough iron coming from your food. The best place to start is with deep-green leafy vegetables, such as spinach and kale. They're loaded with calcium—an element that rarely appears in fruit and vegetables but which is essential for healthy bones and teeth—and with vitamin C, manganese, potassium, and beta-carotene (which is an important nutrient for good vision). Spinach and kale also contain high levels of chlorophyll, a plant pigment present in all green leafy veggies. So eat as many of these lean green delicacies as you can and you will be a healthy, high-powered superbeing!

A fine balance of B vitamins, vitamin C, vitamin E, amino acids, and calcium is important. Eat a good variety of fruit and vegetables—it's easy to get your five-a-day once you get started—and you will feel more balanced and beautiful than ever!

SUPERFOODS

Introducing some superfoods into your diet is also a positive step and can be fun, too. Indigenous people have been eating superfoods like maca and spirulina for thousands of years. So this is an opportunity for you to tap into that ancient knowledge and reap the benefits.

Maca powder comes from a plant that is native to the Andes and has a number of benefits. To start with, it is a great oxygenator of the blood, which helps athletes to perform better (imagine the effect this can have on your studies!). It heightens your immunity, enhances your stamina level, and is a hormonal balancer, great for alleviating menstrual pains. Also, it is an adaptogen, which means it lets the body adapt to many ailments. Maca is also a great natural source of calcium.

Raw cacao is the purest and healthiest way to eat chocolate. It is a natural antidepressant due to the serotonin precursor, tryptophan. (Serotonin is a hormone that plays an important role in the body's regulation of mood, sleep, and anxiety, among other things. Tryptophan is an essential amino acid—which means your body does not produce it and you must get it through diet—that produces serotonin.) It is also the second highest antioxidant food in the world. Furthermore, it has the highest magnesium content of any food.

Spirulina is considered the ultimate superfood. It is a complete protein, containing eight essential amino acids, and has more protein than any other food in the world (very useful for vegetarians in particular). Also high in antioxidants, spirulina contains almost everything we need in the way of vitamins and minerals, in perfect ratios for the human body. Spirulina is also rich in essential fatty acids. For more info on superfoods, check out the website Sun Food Superfoods (www.sunfood.com).

THE BENEFITS OF HOME GARDENING

The next step to becoming healthier is to try growing your own food. And you actually don't need a lot of space to do this. If you have a little garden, it's pretty simple to sow some salad seeds and plant some herbs. Or maybe add a window box for an attractive growing space. If you include some nectar-rich flowers to attract beneficial insects, they'll act as natural predators, feeding on the insects that will attempt to eat your crops before you do!

It's a good idea to build a connection with the plant world and develop a more natural way of being. Plants have a lot of benefits—and why not try sprouting? Experts say that the benefits of sprouted legumes, nuts, and grains are supremely understated. Pound for pound, they are more nutritious than any other food. They can also be eaten fresher than any other food because they grow vigorously right up until the moment when you eat them! Amazingly, sprouts have a complete nutritional profile—which means they can act like a one-stop shop for all your nutritional needs! You can also eat them raw, so they're perfect for anyone on a living-foods diet.

The process of sprouting actually increases the quality, quantity, and variety of nutrients available to us, and it's so easy. So get yourself a sprouting jar. It's a super-cheap way to create an abundance of tasty bean sprouts to eat as salads, or sprinkle over your dishes. They are ready to eat in about three days and make you feel amazing!

Enjoy your journey toward better health—you'll soon be cruising through those academic essays with increased brainpower. With a better relationship with your body, you'll also be on the way to becoming a healthier and happier individual. So invite some friends over, get yourselves in the kitchen, and experiment. Your friends will soon see how exciting, varied, and delicious a healthy diet can be.

Sarah Veniard is a self-employed garden designer, who uses the principles of permaculture in her designs, creating sustainable and environmentally friendly gardens that may produce food and will attract an abundance of beneficial wildlife. You can visit her website at: sarahssecretgarden. wordpress.com.

HOW TO EAT SEASONALLY

BY ANDY GOLD

As a kid, I hated tomatoes. I thought of them as pale, poorly flavored, sad little rocks, completely without life and yet somehow a regular feature of dinners at home for all twelve months of the year. It was only years later, during one particularly bright summer, that I discovered something by the same name that was a delicious delight, ruby red and vibrant yellow, and bursting with juices.

Although both were tomatoes in name, the former was the sad supermarket staple, grown year-round and picked while still green, only turning red later on. Shipped—or worse still—flown to our supermarket shelves, it has become ever present at the disappointing seasonless dinner table. The tasty version was a local variety, picked at the height of summer, in full ripeness, and it had traveled a short distance to my plate. Someone once said to me the best way to learn to dance is just to start dancing, and the same advice works for starting to eat more seasonal food. You'll notice the sheer delight the moment you eat something that is right in season, and you'll find that you won't want to stop.

All seasonal food reminds me of the energizing intensity of a summer holiday. Seasonal tomatoes are delicious for breakfast on toast; at lunchtime in a salad with a drizzle of balsamic vinegar or in a warm dish with shallots, garlic, and some sherry vinegar; or for dinner underneath a whole fresh sardine stuffed full of herbs and lemon. No nights in front of the television, no "I can't be bothered." Just savoring every moment until tomatoes are gone for another year.

Summer is also a great time of year for asparagus. Last year some friends and I did a "pick your own" trip and then cooked the spears quickly in boiling water and then dipped them in soft-boiled eggs. Try it, probably the world's most amazing dippers. Jersey Royal potatoes and artichokes, soon followed in the same season by eggplant and zucchini, are all delicious on the grill with big slices of halloumi cheese. Radishes sprinkled with sea salt go down like small, spicy, savory apples. Or how about crunchy cucumber and watercress sandwiches with bread that's been covered in cream cheese with herbs, garlic, and some hot peppers? And then there are berries, all kinds of wonderful berries, fresh from the bushes, the easiest foraging in the world and perfect for a picnic. As if summer isn't fantastic enough anyway.

There's a reason why all of these fruits and vegetables taste better when you get them locally and in season. Tests show that leafy greens like spinach lose around half of their nutrients in the first twenty-four hours after they're harvested. Along with those nutrients also disappear a lot of the flavor. With all fruit and veggies, it's the same story. The longer it takes to get from field to fork, the less flavorful your mouthful will be. Not only will your taste buds be missing the flavor, your body won't be getting the same nutritious hit of goodness either.

Once you've spent a year enjoying eating seasonally, you'll find yourself starting to look forward to different foods as the seasons change. It's easy enough to look forward to spring and summer, but let's face it, anything that makes us excited about autumn and winter has got to be a good thing. I might curse the first day in October or November that I find myself cycling home in the dark through the rain (or occasionally even snow!), but at least I'm cheered by knowing that when I pass by the grocery store near my house to shop for my dinner, I'll be able to pick up sweet, satisfying parsnips and beets or some aniseed-y fennel for some roasted restoration when I get in the door. It's as if nature knows what I need and has prepared stuff that is best done in the oven, warming up my whole house in the process.

It's wild mushroom and truffle time, too, in autumn. Although I might not be a millionaire (yet!), a summer truffle grated on a poached egg is a part of the millionaire's lifestyle I can afford, if I do the work myself. And summer isn't the end of the great "event" food either; the sexy, sunny days of summer, picnics, and barbecues, give way to warm fires and dark candlelit nights of fondues and feasts.

I ate my first bowl of mussels at the age of twelve. A new tradition—and an event I always look forward to—is building a fire as soon as winter gives way to spring and having a bunch of friends over for big bowls of shellfish cooked in a big iron pan. At this point, I'm also obsessed with oysters and fried squid, too, and prawns from the Atlantic. All are best enjoyed in the cold months and a reason to be cheerful, to get together with friends, and savor winter.

Seasonal food isn't just better for you, tastier, and more fun; it's also cheaper. I work in London now, and recently took a group of my students to one of my favorite places to buy seasonal supplies, the always animated Ridley Road Market, in Hackney, East London. We had a budget big enough for probably a basket's worth of produce from a local supermarket, yet somehow we emerged from the Ridley Road Market with bags upon bags of fresh fruit—all at a staggeringly low price. Admittedly, we had some help from Tony, who's in charge of the fruit and vegetables there.

"How come it's so cheap?" one of my students asked (with her jaw on the floor, I should add).

"Yesterday that sweet corn was in the ground in Essex, just outside London," explained Tony. "There's no trick to growing it," he continued. "It just needs some land and some patience. In the afternoon a van came by and a load of corn was picked and put on the back of it and driven into town. I picked it up first thing this morning and now it's here with you in time for you to take some home for lunch. It's cheap because it's simple and no one's had to do too much work to get it here."

But no matter where you live, there are local markets near you with traders just like Tony. As an added bonus, if you become a regular face at someone's stall, you'll probably start getting the benefit of discounts and other juicy bonuses. Support your local vendors, and they'll remember you better than a corporate loyalty card ever can.

In the big picture, we all understand how reducing our carbon footprint is good for the planet and really important if we don't want to see the earth's climate changing at a more alarming rate than it already is. You don't need to be a rocket scientist to work out that more local, seasonal food means less energy spent transporting produce around.

Whenever you're reading this, I can guarantee that whatever the season, there will be something amazing in the shops. To find out what's getting us excited today, check out our website, and while you're online you can add to the fantastic recipes in this book by searching for some new ideas yourself.

Andy Gold *is a chef and cooking teacher. He works for* *Shoreditch Trust, managing the Blue Marble Training* *Program, which helps people with ambition, a passion for* *food, and untapped potential to find careers in the food* *industry. To learn more about Blue Marble Training, visit* *www.shoreditchtrust.org.uk/Blue-Marble-Training.*

EATING ORGANIC

BY CHLOE HARRIS

To go organic or not? Is it healthier and more nutritious? Or simply tastier? Is the whole thing a scam to get you to pay more for nothing? How do you decide?

The first thing we need to understand is just how organic food is different. Food can only be certified as organic if it follows certain rules of production (look for the green USDA Organic symbol on packaged food). Organic farmers are allowed to use only a limited number of pesticides, but no chemical fertilizers. They develop soil that is rich in nutrients by natural means, such as rotating crops, and they encourage insects and other wildlife to help reduce the number of pests. Organic farming is definitely kinder to the environment.

Many people now agree that on factory farms—where animals are treated like commodities and usually endure poor living conditions—the food that is produced is not going to be of the best quality. In contrast, organic farmers treat animals humanely and do not use drugs such as antibiotics or worming agents. Instead, farmers must find natural ways of keeping the animals healthy. The use of genetically modified organisms (GMOs) is also prohibited on organic farms. According to many pro-organic farmers and consumers, all these factors result in organic food being more nutritious and having a wonderful fresh and tasty flavor, compared with the bland taste of nonorganic products. Organic farming scores well, too, with its respect for living creatures.

Organic food is not processed with colorants, additives, preservatives, or irradiation. As some people are sensitive to or have adverse reactions to these processes and additives, organic food is a safer bet for people with allergies.

So what's not to like? The biggest disadvantage is the *cost* of organic food. As it is more expensive to produce, it's costlier to buy. Organic food also lasts a shorter time than nonorganic food, as it contains no preservatives. This means it goes to waste if it's not used quickly. This adds to the cost for farmers and shops that sell organic products, and it raises the price for consumers. In addition to the cost, many scientists deny there are *any* health or nutritional benefits: "Current evidence shows that organic food is not significantly different in terms of nutrition from food produced conventionally" (FSA Study/London School of Hygiene & Tropical Medicine, 2009). So it's hard for the individual to know what to believe.

A more cost-effective way of going organic is to grow your own food. My family has tried this in our own garden. We've grown beans and asparagus, and they were both delicious! Homegrown organic food tastes better and obviously costs less than buying it from the shops. Growing your own food is also a great way of minimizing waste. It means you're more likely to eat food quickly, so that it does not go bad. If you have a garden, you're already halfway there! Or maybe there's a community garden near you that you can become involved with. There are many books and websites on organic gardening to assist you. In my quest to find out more about organic food, I asked some people in my hometown what they think of the issue:

Seventeen-year-old Nitin Patel says, "In my household we like to buy organic occasionally since it tastes better and is better for the environment. When I get my own place, I will carry on buying organic. I find that if you choose your products wisely, stop over-eating, and don't buy ready-made products that cost loads of money, buying organic food isn't much more expensive than eating unhealthy cheap food in the end. But you need to learn how to eat properly again, and for some of us, it's not easy."

Thirty-three-year-old Wayne Brown says, "I like the taste of organic food, and I like to splurge once in a while but could not afford to eat organic every day. On top of that, I'm not even sure it's better for your health. And they say that you can never really know what is organic and what isn't. Because if you've got an organic crop in one field and a nonorganic crop in the next one, the wind can blow the nonorganic seeds toward the organic field. I hear that a lot. I don't know if it's true, but it makes sense. And it makes me doubt the very concept of organic food."

Sixty-year-old Pamela Ross says, "I have heard that organic food is better for the environment. And I think it's a good idea to treat animals well, rather than make them suffer just so that we can afford to eat them! I think organic farming is a good thing,

and I eat organic meat and milk at the least. Some say that organic food isn't really better for you. Maybe it isn't. So what? Treating the animals and nature more humanely is a good enough reason to buy organic food, isn't it? The way we grow food nowadays and the way we treat animals is shameful. If organic farming can change that, whether better for health or not, I don't care. It's a good thing, anyway."

Nineteen-year-old Sally Smith says, "It's just too expensive! I'm strapped for cash most of the time and would rather spend my disposable income on going out with my friends!"

So where are you on the organic spectrum? Total nonorganic consumer? A little, occasionally? Or full-blown organic all the time? Most people seem to be hovering around the middle. At the end of the day, it's up to you, but I hope I have helped you weigh the pros and cons to make up your own mind.

Chloe Harris is currently attending high school. She is really into cooking, especially her favorite food: pear sorbet. She has three dogs and two cats.

VEGETARIANISM

BY SHERRY WEST

Vegetarianism, of course, is as old as the hills. Most people in India are vegetarians, since both Hindus and Jains espouse a vegetarian diet and a philosophy of nonviolence toward animals. For millennia, a large proportion, if not a majority, of the human race has chosen to forego meat and fish in favor of vegetables.

Our ancestors were hunter-gatherers who ate mostly fruit and berries, roots and grubs, with the occasional addition of mammoth, kangaroo, and alligator. Like chimpanzees, we have evolved to feed omnivorously. Our teeth and digestive system still testify to this fact.

However, once people took up farming and gained a surplus of food, mere survival was supplanted by lifestyle choices. Today, vegetarianism remains mainly a lifestyle choice, although people choose it for a variety of reasons —religious, political, economic, cultural, as well as for health.

Certainly, it's not hard to stay healthy without meat. A reasonable variety of fruit, vegetables, legumes, nuts, oils, and eggs and dairy products (if included in the diet) will provide everything the body needs. The careful vegetarian can easily get all the protein, fat, carbohydrates, vitamins, minerals, and amino acids that he or she will need.

Vegetarians tend to have lower cholesterol, lower blood pressure, and fewer diseases than meat eaters. Studies show that a vegetarian diet is less likely to result in heart disease, diabetes, colon cancer, and obesity than one that includes meat. There is also less risk of food contamination (although the outbreak of *E. coli* in northern Germany in 2011 shows that plant foods such as lettuce and bean sprouts can be sources, too). Eggs are common sources of salmonella.

Some vegetarians eat dairy products and eggs, and others will also eat fish and seafood. Vegans, on the other hand, refuse food that contains *any* animal products. They may also refuse to wear clothing that is made from animals or contains products, chemicals, or dyes tested on animals.

Many argue that vegetarianism is more environmentally friendly, too. The vast increase in cattle herds for the beef market has led to a huge amount of land being given over to cattle, rather than to growing food plants and trees. In addition, the incredible amount of methane that cows release adds to the buildup of greenhouse gases in the atmosphere each year. Equally, the demand for fish has depleted their populations in the oceans and affected marine ecosystems in many parts of the world, bringing many species to the point of extinction.

So why not try going vegetarian? First, be aware that when you stop eating meat—and fish, if you choose to give it up—your body will naturally crave it. This is when it is important to be strong and persist. A vital part of this process is ensuring that you are replacing all the vitamins, minerals, and nutrients that you once got from meat and fish with vegetarian alternatives.

Meat provides a lot of protein, though not in a form that our bodies can absorb easily. It is also very difficult for us to break down meat, so the digestive process is extremely slow, which can lead to feelings of low energy and heaviness. It is advisable to replace this protein source with veggie alternatives, such as soy products like tofu or tempeh.

Other great sources of protein include beans and other legumes and nuts. Why not make sumptuous falafel balls and serve them with warm pita bread, salad, and natural yogurt? Or transport your new experimental cuisine to India and make a lentil dal topped with cashews and served with rice and greens. There are many good alternatives to good old pasta and pizza, including noodles, couscous, and wild rice. For more ideas, see the recipes in this book or check out websites such as the Vegetarian Times (www.vegetariantimes.com).

FLEXITARIAN

For those of you who can't give up meat altogether, try cutting down to a couple of times a week, and alternate between meat, fish, and vegetable-based main dishes. A good plan is to eat less meat and fish, and when you do eat them, spend a little more on organic options, which are not processed and pumped full of chemicals and additives.

When it comes to fish, be careful which fish you choose, as Atlantic cod, haddock, bluefin tuna, and orange roughy are on the endangered list. As a result of fishing quotas, fishermen discard almost a quarter of their catch because the fish are the wrong species. Meanwhile, deep-sea trawlers are removing an unsustainable number of bottom-dwelling fish—which don't even start breeding until they are twenty to thirty years old—decimating fish stocks. To find out more, check out the red list on the Greenpeace website (www.greenpeace.org/international/seafood).

Finally, I hope I've helped you realize that your choice of food is not simply a personal matter but a political and moral choice. It affects the environment, farmers, and fishermen in other parts of the world, and most of all, the lives and future of other living creatures.

Sherry West has a degree in cooking from Darlington College and now runs a whole-food café in the U.K.

HOW TO EAT LOCALLY

BY EDWARD GOSLING

California oranges? Tuna from coastal Chile? Lamb from New Zealand? Avocados from Spain? Mangoes from Pakistan? Coffee from Kenya? The world is on your doorstep. Push your shopping cart down the aisles, and take your pick, right? It's all so shiny looking—different colors, exotic food. You can buy strawberries in winter, apples all year round. Supermarkets certainly seem to be offering us more diverse options from, well, just about everywhere! But can we rest easy in our eating, or does this greater choice come at a cost?

There's an obvious reason why eating locally produced food is better—it has a far lower environmental impact. In order to get all those foods from all over the world onto your plate, a lot of fossil fuels are burned every day. Try the 100-mile diet, which is a commitment to only eat foods produced within 100 miles of your home, so you can rest assured that the food you're eating is adding very little to your carbon footprint. Eating local produce keeps you connected to the seasons, as you are eating only what's available. This might even push you to experiment a bit and try some new things, instead of just resorting to that tried-and-true dish you make on autopilot. Your food is also going to be a lot fresher. Local fruit and vegetables can stay in the ground or on the tree those extra few days, which is when they really soak up loads of flavor and nutrients. It's not only healthier for you, but poses less risk—food transported long distances has a much higher chance of becoming contaminated.

At a time when globalization is trying to suck us up into its oh-so-tempting giant, homogenous, unquestioning approach to the world (get more stuff, buy the same things, look the same, be the same, obey, obey, obey), eating locally does something positive for the community around you. Buying straight from farmers on your doorstep supports the local economy, which may mean you get that money back more easily, so you're really helping to support yourself. By choosing locally grown food, you're helping to preserve green spaces—farmland—from development, and it cuts out the middleman.

Why give faceless supermarkets all the cash? Why not instead meet people who care about the food they're growing because it's their livelihood? Giving local farmers money directly restores the relationship between the consumer and the supplier and gives you a personal connection with a grower. And you don't just support farmers in the United States; you also support farmers and consumers in developing countries. If a consumer in the US is willing to buy an African or South American farmer's produce at a higher price than local people will give him, the farmer is obviously going to sell at a higher price. Hey, he's got a wife to support, kids to educate, a couple of debts to pay off. But this can mean that people in developing countries have to pay inflated prices for food that is produced locally for them, which really isn't very fair.

If you are feeling bad for the farmer in the developing world, think something like this: It's a capitalist free market economy. Why should we expect him to accept less than he can get for his crop? What right do we have to interfere? Then you should know that many farms in developing countries are now owned by large companies or banks. Attracted by the financial opportunities that can be made by buying up vast tracts of cheap land, exploiting expendable, unregulated labor, and selling off produce to richer countries, they reap huge profits. The economies of scale they're able to implement mean small farmers can't compete and are forced to sell off their land, perpetuating an oppressive system further. The farmers then work on these massive estates for a pitiful wage. So the rich get richer, food prices go up, more people starve, and you get food that isn't as fresh and tasty as you could get if you just went two miles down the road. This is a lose-lose-lose situation. Don't be a part of it.

When you go to the supermarket, it may seem like you're getting more choice, but appearances can be deceiving. How many types of apples can you name? Granny Smith, Red Delicious, Fuji...? Did you know that there are over 7,500 different types of apple in the world? In the nineteenth century, among the thousands of apple varieties you could choose from in the U.K., you could get the Hoary Morning, Blenheim Orange, Knobby Russet, and Laxton's Epicure. Today, a huge proportion of the apples that the British eat come from overseas. What happened? Well, small shops turned into large chains and they stopped buying local produce. All those delicious apple varieties weren't valued, and instead giant orchards with mile after mile of the same variety took over to cater to big retailers. How boring!

Recent studies have shown that eating locally is better for air quality and lowering pollution than eating organically. And—a big thing to think about—it is also much cheaper. When you eat locally produced food, you don't have to pay for transportation, fuel, the truck driver's wage, or for all the people handling and packaging the food. Food prices are rising above inflation around the world, so for me, spending less on my weekly shopping is a hell of an incentive, especially when I'm helping out the environment, local farmers, and people around the world—and getting something fresher, tastier, and more healthful, all at the same time.

Edward Gosling is an editor and circus performer, which means he likes to read and also to play with fire. He has a habit of accidentally cooking food for fifteen people. He's currently cooking a lot of red cabbage.

WHAT IS FAIRTRADE?

BY BARRY HALLINGER

The fairtrade movement, which began in the 1960s, aimed to create a system to combat the inherent inequalities rife in the world trading system. By paying unrealistically low prices for products to increase consumer interest, companies in "developed" countries discriminated against producer countries, which usually had much lower national wealth. In the 1970s and '80s, competitive trading resulted in price deflation, whereby companies lowered the prices of their products to compete in a supply-and-demand market. According to the Fair Trade Advocacy Office, "The total loss for developing countries, due to falling commodity prices, has been estimated by the Food and Agricultural Organization [of the United Nations] to total almost $250 billion during the 1980 to 2002 period." The people most seriously affected were agricultural farmers, who had to procure more land to grow and increase output—usually for no financial gain.

Fairtrade certification is for products that sell at above market price with the aim that the extra money is to go directly to the farmers and their communities. These better prices improve working conditions, reduce child labor, and increase the sustainability of trade in the long term. Fairtrade products also support development projects, such as the building of schools and hospitals, and reduce the environmental impact from poor farming practices. If you buy fairtrade products, you are standing up for basic human rights and sending the message that it is not acceptable to ignore the rights of producers who suffer from the conventional trading system.

The fairtrade program is an attempt to address these market failures by providing farmers and producers with a reasonable price for their crop, as well as business advice, access to the "developing" nation markets, and better trading conditions.

You might think that you cannot afford the extra cash for that bag of coffee. But in reality, current market prices do not properly reflect the true costs associated with production, and only a well-managed, stable minimum-price system can cover environmental and social production costs. And that is the aim of the fairtrade certification scheme.

However, while the fairtrade movement is a monumental step in the right direction against the consolidation of wealth for a few, and is actively campaigning for basic human rights and sustainable development, it is not without its critics. It is argued that paying more for products creates a false subsidy that harms farmers in the long term, and that it prevents what is really needed—a fundamental change in the trading system. This, in my opinion, is something that must be addressed if the movement itself wants to be fully legitimate and sustainable. There is a lack of evidence demonstrating that participating in the scheme produces a net positive economic result for fairtrade product suppliers. It may, in fact, have a negative effect on non-fairtrade farmers.

From the time fairtrade was introduced, there are few reliable studies attempting to measure impacts on fairtrade farmers and a control of matched non-fairtrade farmers. Also, there appears to be none assessing which of the many aid organizations involved is responsible for any changes observed. This failure of fairtrade monitoring organizations— Fairtrade International (FLO) and FLO-Cert, which inspects and certifies fairtrade producers—to check the social, economical, and environmental benefits of producer countries, raises questions of why the companies are still not transparent and challenges the legitimacy of the various umbrella companies that regulate it.

Although these are big issues that must be addressed in the coming years, philosophically and practically, fairtrade is a beneficial trading system for the future sustainability of the human race. Consumption should be based on production, not false market competition, and workers, no matter where, should benefit from their hard work, see their communities grow, and not be exploited so you can save a few pennies on a bunch of bananas.

If you agree with the principle and practice of fairtrade certification, you can check which products are available locally to you on the Fairtade International website (www.fairtrade.net).

Barry Hallinger *graduated in 2009 with a bachelor of arts in social anthropology and helped build a school and teach English in the Nepalese Himalayas. He has started a community-based project called Ethnogenic, which supports friend-based markets and raises money for charity projects. He is inspired to try and create a more realistic and fair economy by removing the artificial distance between producer and supplier of commodities. He plans to get a masters degree in international relations and environmental law.*

DIY KITCHEN STAPLES

BEANS, TWO WAYS

MAKES 3 CUPS

QUICK BEANS

2.5 HRS

INGREDIENTS

1 cup dried beans

1 bay leaf

1 garlic clove

1 tablespoon chopped fresh parsley or another fresh herb

1/3 cup vegetable ends or chopped vegetables, such as onions, carrots, or celery

1 tablespoon extra-virgin olive oil

Salt and pepper

Put the beans in a large pot and cover with 4 to 5 inches of water. Cover the pot and bring to a boil. Remove from the heat and let the beans sit, covered, for 1 hour.

Drain the pot and cover with 2 to 3 inches of fresh water. Add the remaining ingredients and bring back to a boil, uncovered. Lower the heat and simmer until the beans reach the desired consistency. Plan for around 1 hour, but the cooking time for each type of bean differs.

SOAKED OVERNIGHT

9.5 HRS

Follow the above recipe, but instead of letting the beans sit in hot water for 1 hour, soak in room temperature water, covered, overnight.

QUICK TIPS The beans will take on whatever flavors you add to the water. Don't like parsley? Use oregano instead. Can't get enough cheese? Add a rind of your favorite Parmesan instead of throwing it out. Want smoky beans? Add black peppercorns, paprika, and bacon. ✳ Beans are an amazing way to get the most nutritional bang for your buck. Make a large batch of beans over the weekend and enjoy them all week long, any time of day. For breakfast, top a piece of toast with last night's leftover veggies, a handful of beans, and a soft-boiled egg; drizzle with olive oil. For lunch, top a bowl of beans with chopped bell peppers and crumbled feta or goat cheese. For dinner, toss a handful of beans in your soup or salad, or wrap in a tortilla with leftover chicken or shrimp. Remember, one pound of dried beans will make about 6 cups of cooked beans, and will cost you about $2.00.

VINAIGRETTE DRESSING

10 MINS : MAKES 1 CUP

INGREDIENTS

⅔ cup extra-virgin olive oil

¼ cup good-quality vinegar

1 teaspoon Dijon mustard

½ teaspoon salt

¼ teaspoon ground pepper

Pinch of sugar

Combine all the ingredients in a small bowl and whisk together or blend with a hand blender. You can add a pinch of sugar if you like it less sharp. The mixture will keep in a refrigerated, covered container for 2 weeks. Mix or shake well before using.

> QUICK TIP   For a vinaigrette with a bit more bite, add 1 to 2 tablespoons of minced shallots.

BÉCHAMEL SAUCE

15 MINS : MAKES 2¼ CUPS

INGREDIENTS

2 cups whole milk

2 tablespoons butter

2 tablespoons all-purpose flour

¼ teaspoon grated nutmeg

Salt and pepper

Heat the milk in a medium saucepan over medium-high heat until nearly boiling. Melt the butter in another medium saucepan over medium-low heat. Add the flour to the pan with the butter and stir for 2 minutes until the mixture turns blond. This is called a *roux*. Add one ladleful of milk at a time to the *roux*, stirring until it's smooth. Repeat until all the milk has been added. Season with the nutmeg, salt, and pepper. You can add grated cheese at this stage for a cheese sauce, or herbs or spices. Once cooled, place plastic wrap against the surface of the sauce so it doesn't form a skin. It will keep in the fridge for 2 days. Reheat with a dash of milk and stir until smooth.

TOMATO SAUCE

(fresh tomatoes in the summer, canned in the winter)

45 MINS : MAKES 5 CUPS

INGREDIENTS

¼ cup extra-virgin olive oil

1 medium onion, diced

¼ teaspoon red pepper flakes

1 garlic clove, minced

⅓ cup white wine

2¼ pounds medium-ripe tomatoes (usually about 8), cut into quarters (see Quick Tips)

Heat the olive oil in a large saucepan over medium heat. Add the onion and cook until translucent, about 5 minutes. Add the red pepper flakes and garlic and cook, stirring, for 1 minute. Add the wine and tomatoes and cook for 20 minutes, stirring occasionally. At this point, you can leave as is for a chunky tomato sauce or pass the ingredients through a sieve or blend in a food processor or blender for a fine tomato sauce. Or cook for an additional 10 minutes, blend, and serve as tomato soup!

> QUICK TIPS Only use fresh tomatoes in the summer, when they are ripe and in season. In the winter months, the fresh tomatoes can be replaced with cans of whole, peeled tomatoes. Reserve the juice until the end of the recipe. If you feel your sauce is too thick, add the juice ¼ cup at a time and stir until the desired consistency is reached. ※ If serving with pasta, stir in ¼ cup roughly chopped fresh herbs, such as basil and parsley.

PESTO

15 MINS : MAKES 1 CUP

INGREDIENTS

2 cups packed fresh basil leaves (see Quick Tip)

About ⅔ cup extra-virgin olive oil

½ cup grated Parmesan cheese

⅓ cup pine nuts

2 to 3 garlic cloves, minced

Salt and pepper

Blend the basil and 1 tablespoon of the olive oil in a blender or food processor until broken down. Add the Parmesan cheese, pine nuts, and garlic and blend, while slowly adding the remaining oil. Stop adding oil when the pesto reaches the desired consistency. Taste and season with salt and pepper.

> QUICK TIP If basil isn't in season, substitute another flavorful leafy green, such as parsley, arugula, cilantro, or a mix of what you have in the fridge.

SALSA

45 MINS : MAKES 1¹/₅ CUPS

INGREDIENTS

2 ripe tomatoes, diced
2 jalapeño chiles, diced
½ medium onion, diced
1 handful fresh cilantro, chopped
1½ to 2 tablespoons fresh lemon or lime juice
Salt and pepper

Toss together the tomatoes, jalapeños, onion, cilantro, and lemon or lime juice in a large bowl. Season with salt and pepper. Chill in the refrigerator for at least 30 minutes and then enjoy! The salsa will keep chilled and covered up to 5 days.

QUICK TIP Sure, everyone knows that salsa goes great with tortilla chips, but there are many other ways to enjoy this fresh tomato treat: Spoon over steak or pork chops, or serve with fish instead of chimichurri sauce (see page 98). Or consider kicking your breakfast up a notch by topping scrambled eggs with a couple of spoonfuls of this fresh salsa. ✳ If you're not a fan of spicy salsa, leave out the jalapeños in the recipe and use diced green bell peppers instead.

MAYONNAISE

15 MINS : MAKES 1¼ CUPS

INGREDIENTS

1 large egg yolk, room temperature
1 teaspoon fresh lemon juice
1 teaspoon water
¼ teaspoon Dijon mustard
¾ cup good-quality canola oil, plus more as needed
Salt

In a chilled medium bowl, whisk the egg yolk, lemon juice, water, and mustard until it blends together. Continue whisking, and slowly add the oil in a thin, steady pour, ½ teaspoon at a time, until the mayonnaise has a thick consistency. If the mayonnaise is not the desired consistency after adding ¾ cup of oil, add a little more, slowly, until the desired consistency is reached. Stir in salt to taste. Refrigerate if not using immediately.

VEGETABLE STOCK

2 HRS | MAKES 2 QUARTS

INGREDIENTS

2 tablespoons extra-virgin olive oil
5 to 6 garlic cloves
2 to 3 carrots, chopped
2 parsnips, chopped
2 celery stalks, chopped
1 onion, chopped
1 bunch parsley
3 sprigs thyme
1 bay leaf
5 to 6 whole peppercorns

Heat the oil in a stockpot over medium heat. Add the garlic, carrots, parsnips, celery, and onion. Cook until softened, about 10 to 15 minutes.

Pour about 3 quarts of water into the stockpot. Add the remaining ingredients. Bring to a boil, lower the heat, and simmer for about 1 hour. Let cool and pour the stock through a strainer. Discard the vegetables.

Use immediately or store in the refrigerator for up to 1 week or in the freezer for up to 3 months.

QUICK TIP Save money by storing vegetable trimmings (carrot tops, potato skins, and celery leaves, for example) in the freezer and then using them in the stock, instead of fresh vegetables. Also, feel free to replace the ingredients with vegetables you have on hand.

CHICKEN STOCK

5.5 HRS | MAKES 2 QUARTS

INGREDIENTS

4½ pounds raw or cooked chicken bones or carcasses, without skin
5 carrots
5 whole peppercorns
3 garlic cloves
3 sprigs parsley
2 medium onions
2 celery stalks
1 leek
1 sprig thyme
1 bay leaf

Put all of the ingredients into a stockpot and cover with water. Bring to a boil over medium-high heat. Once the water comes to a boil, turn the heat down to low and simmer for 3 to 5 hours, until the stock is as flavorful as you like. While it's simmering, occasionally skim any foam or oil that rises to the top; this will keep the stock clear and clean tasting. Strain the broth and cool. Use immediately or store in the refrigerator for up to 1 week or in the freezer for up to 3 months.

QUICK TIPS Try asking your local butcher for chicken carcasses, he may even give you them for free! Another option is to store leftover chicken bones/carcasses in the freezer until you have enough to make a broth. ※ To make beef stock, follow this recipe, substituting beef bones for chicken bones.

PEANUT BUTTER

40 MINS ⋮ MAKES ³/₄ CUP

INGREDIENTS

2 to 3 cups peanuts, shelled

¼ cup plus 2 tablespoons peanut oil (sunflower or
    safflower oil will also work)

Salt or sugar

Preheat the oven to 350°F. Place the nuts on a lightly greased baking sheet and cook for 15 to 20 minutes. Stir once or twice during the cooking time. When the peanuts are cooked, let them cool for about 10 minutes. Then rub them between your fingers to take off their thin, brown skins, which should come off easily. Put the peanuts in a food processor and add the oil. Blend well. You can add some sugar or salt to taste, if you want sweet or savory peanut butter. Or you can just have it as it is. Store in an airtight container in the refrigerator for 2 months. Enjoy!

CHOCOLATE SPREAD

30 MINS ⋮ MAKES 4 CUPS

INGREDIENTS

1 cup roasted hazelnuts

4 ounces dark chocolate, broken up

7 ounces milk chocolate, broken up

1¾ cups whole milk

¼ cup powdered skim milk

3 tablespoons honey

¼ teaspoon salt

Process the hazelnuts in a food processor or blender until in powder form. Melt the dark and milk chocolate in the top of a double boiler over simmering water. Or melt in a microwave-safe bowl in the microwave. If using the microwave, give the chocolate a stir every 30 seconds to prevent it from burning; continue until fully melted. Add the nut powder to the melted chocolate and stir until everything is mixed together. Scrape the chocolate from the sides of the food bowl if it sticks.

Bring the whole milk, powdered skim milk, honey, and salt to a boil in a medium saucepan. Add to the food processor and process until smooth. If the mixture looks runny, don't worry. Once the chocolate starts to cool, the spread will thicken. Store the chocolate spread in an airtight container or jar with a screw top (think peanut butter). The spread will keep for up to 4 days at room temperature or 4 weeks in the refrigerator.

Chapter

3

. . . .

BREAKFAST AND BRUNCH

GRANOLA

BY MAIA HACKETT

"The best thing about making granola at home is that you don't need to worry about being exact in measurements or ingredients – you can use up any seeds, nuts, or fruits you find in your pantry."

1.25 HRS : MAKES 5 CUPS

INGREDIENTS

4 cups old-fashioned rolled oats (not instant)

1 cup raw nuts (almonds, pecans, walnuts, cashews, hazelnuts—you decide!), chopped

½ cup raw seeds (sunflower, pumpkin, sesame, flax—you decide!)

½ teaspoon ground cinnamon

¾ teaspoon fine sea salt

¼ cup honey

⅓ cup vegetable oil

½ cup packed light brown sugar

1 teaspoon vanilla extract

1 cup unsweetened dried fruit (raisins, cranberries, cherries, apricots—you decide!), chopped

Preheat the oven to 300°F.

In a large mixing bowl, stir together the oats, nuts, seeds, cinnamon, and salt. Set aside.

In a small saucepan, combine the honey, vegetable oil, and sugar. Bring to a boil over medium heat, stirring constantly. Remove from the heat, allow to cool, and stir in the vanilla. Pour the syrup mixture over the oats mixture and stir with a wooden spoon to coat evenly.

Spread the mixture on a baking sheet lined with parchment paper and bake for 15 minutes. Stir and bake until the granola is a light golden brown, about 15 to 20 more minutes. (Keep an eye on it! All ovens are different, and you don't want it to burn.)

Allow to cool for about 20 minutes, stirring occasionally—the granola will harden as it cools. Stir in the dried fruit and serve. This granola can be kept in an airtight container in a cool, dry place for up to 2 weeks.

> QUICK TIP Substitute maple syrup for the honey for a different flavor. Also try ginger, nutmeg, and even cardamom, if you like spicier fare! ※ Granola is good as a go-to snack or as a topper for yogurt.

YOGURT MUESLI

BY SONIA GIN FIZ

"Waking up in the morning is not an easy task for me. That's why I like breakfasts that are both tasty and easy to make. And I think this one is a very good example."

10 MINS : SERVES 1

INGREDIENTS

4 to 5 strawberries
1 cup yogurt or soy yogurt
⅓ cup dried fruit, such as mangoes and bananas
¼ cup of rice puffs
¼ cup of old-fashioned rolled oats (not instant)
Sweetener, such as sugar, honey, or agave syrup (optional)

Put the yogurt and strawberries in a medium bowl. Mash together with a fork until they're well blended and the yogurt is pink. Add the dried fruit, rice puffs, and oats.

And that's it! If the strawberries are ripe, you don't even need to add sugar. But if you want extra sweetness, you can add some honey or agave syrup.

This recipe works well with all kinds of cereal foods and all kinds of dried fruit, but this combination happens to be my favorite.

ENERGY BAR

BY ELLY PRADINAT

" Energy bars are perfect for hiking, when you've got tests, or when you just need rich, easy food. But the bars they sell in supermarkets are often packed with preservatives, and that's why I like to make my own. You can adapt the bars to your taste and choose your favorite fruits, nuts, and cereal!"

4 HRS | MAKES ABOUT 5 BARS

QUICK TIP To crush almonds, pulse them in a food processor or coffee bean grinder until they reach the desired consistency. If you don't have a food processor or coffee bean grinder, you can put them in a plastic bag and crush with a rolling pin or meat tenderizer.

INGREDIENTS

½ cup (1 stick) butter

3½ tablespoons sugar

3½ tablespoons honey

½ cup cereal of your choice

½ cup almonds, crushed (see Quick Tip)

½ cup dried fruit

Preheat the oven to 325°F.

Combine the butter, sugar, and honey in a medium saucepan over medium heat. Stir continuously until the butter has melted and the sugar and honey have dissolved. Add the cereal, crushed almonds, and dried fruit and stir to blend. Remove from heat and let thicken for a few minutes.

After the mixture has thickened, spread it out evenly in a square baking pan, preferably nonstick, pressing the mixture into the pan. Put it in the oven and bake for about 25 minutes.

Let cool in the pan in the refrigerator for a few hours. Once the mixture has cooled completely, cut into bar-size pieces, wrap in plastic wrap, and store in the refrigerator. They'll keep for up to 1 week!

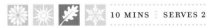

BANANA SMOOTHIE

BY ALEX MCKECHNIE

" My milkshake brings all the boys (and girls) to the backyard — and they're absolutely right about it being better than yours! He he he he he!"

10 MINS : SERVES 2

INGREDIENTS

2 scoops frozen yogurt
1¼ cups milk
1 banana
3½ tablespoons honey
½ teaspoon ground nutmeg

Well . . . not much of a method here. Just take everything and put it in the blender.

Blend and drink! What else?

QUICK TIP   If this smoothie is too sweet for you, omit the nutmeg and use 1 avocado instead of the banana. The consistency of the smoothie will be just as creamy, but the flavor will be less sweet. On the other hand, if you have an extreme sweet tooth, use an extra-ripe banana.

VEGETABLE SMOOTHIE

BY BARRY HALLINGER

" Vegetables, vegetables, vegetables – I love vegetables! In juices, in cakes, every-where. They are full of vitamins and they taste great. In a smoothie they're even better, as you're eating them raw. A good way to get your five a day!"

10 MINS : SERVES 1

INGREDIENTS

1 carrot, peeled and chopped
1 cucumber, peeled and chopped
1 orange, peeled and chopped
1 tomato, chopped
1 apple, peeled and chopped
1½ teaspoons honey
Juice of ½ lemon

Put the carrot, cucumber, orange, tomato, apple, and honey in a blender. Blend for a few minutes until liquefied. Squeeze in the lemon juice, stir, and refrigerate until cold.

QUICK TIP   For vegetarians looking for ways to add more iron into their diets, add a handful of fresh spinach to this smoothie.

FRENCH TOAST

BY NICHOLAS ST. MELUC

" In France, we call this pain perdu (which means " lost bread ") because we use stale bread to make it. So it's a good recipe to know, because you keep your old bread and turn it into a delicious breakfast!"

 35 MINS : SERVES 2

INGREDIENTS

2 large eggs
1 cup milk
2 tablespoons sugar, plus more as needed
4 stale bread slices
1 tablespoon cooking oil

Whisk the eggs in a shallow dish. In another shallow dish, whisk the milk and sugar until blended.

Soak each slice of bread in the eggs, one at a time, for about 2 minutes on each side. Then soak each slice of bread in the milk for 2 minutes per side.

When the first two slices are ready, warm a little bit of oil in a frying pan over medium heat. Cook the slices, two at a time, for about 2 minutes on each side, or until they turn golden brown. Before you flip the bread in the pan, sprinkle with a little bit of sugar, depending on how sweet you prefer your French toast.

It's ready!

PUMPKIN PANCAKES

BY STEPHEN SPANGLER

"I really like pumpkin muffins, so I tried pumpkin pancakes. These are really good and easy to make. I don't even use butter or syrup!"

35 MINS : SERVES 4–5

INGREDIENTS

1 cup all-purpose flour

¼ cup brown sugar

1½ teaspoons baking powder

½ teaspoon salt

½ teaspoon ground cinnamon

½ teaspoon ground ginger

½ teaspoon ground nutmeg

1 cup milk

⅓ cup pumpkin purée (see Quick Tip)

1 large egg

1 tablespoon canola oil

1 teaspoon vanilla extract

Butter to coat the pan

Maple syrup, jam, honey, or whipped cream for serving

In a large bowl, whisk together the flour, sugar, baking powder, salt, cinnamon, ginger, and nutmeg. In a medium bowl, whisk the milk, pumpkin purée, egg, canola oil, and vanilla until uniform in texture. Fold the wet mixture into the dry mixture until well incorporated.

Heat a frying pan or griddle over medium-high heat, and add enough butter to coat the pan. Once the butter has melted, reduce the heat to medium. For regular-size pancakes, drop ¼ cup of batter onto the pan; for silver dollar pancakes, use about 2 tablespoons of batter per pancake. Flip the pancake after about 2 minutes, or when the edges appear to be firm. Cook the second side for another minute, or until golden brown.

Serve warm with syrup, jam, honey, or whipped cream.

QUICK TIP To make pumpkin purée, chop a pumpkin in half and remove the seeds. Lightly sprinkle with salt and place flesh-side-down on a parchment-lined or oiled baking sheet. Bake in a 375°F oven for 40 to 45 minutes, or until you can easily pierce through the skin with a fork in several places. Scoop out the flesh, and blend until smooth in a blender or food processor. The pumpkin purée will keep covered in the fridge for 5 to 7 days, or 3 months in the freezer. Homemade pumpkin purée tastes better than canned, but canned will work in a pinch.

CHICKEN AND WAFFLES

BY ISABELLA FROST

"Who doesn't love fried chicken and waffles? This Southern treat is great for a Sunday brunch with your friends."

1.25 HRS : SERVES 4–6

INGREDIENTS

For the Chicken
1 cup milk
2 large eggs
2 cups all-purpose flour
1 teaspoon paprika
1 tablespoon salt
1 teaspoon pepper
1 chicken, cut into 8 pieces (or 8 pieces of your favorite chicken part)
Vegetable oil for frying

For the Waffles
2 cups all-purpose flour
1 teaspoon baking powder
1 teaspoon salt
1 teaspoon sugar
1 teaspoon baking soda
2 cups buttermilk
1 large egg, beaten
4 tablespoons butter, melted
Maple syrup (optional)

To make the chicken: Whisk the milk and eggs in a shallow bowl. Mix the flour, paprika, salt, and pepper in another shallow bowl. Dip each chicken piece into the milk mixture, letting the excess milk drip back into the bowl. Then dredge in the flour mixture, shaking the excess back into the bowl.

Fill a large pan with high sides with about 1 inch of vegetable oil. Heat the oil over medium-high heat until very hot. Fry the chicken pieces in batches, about 8 to 10 minutes on each side, or until golden brown. Be careful not to flip too early! (If you need to add more oil, make sure it gets hot again.) Check for doneness by piercing with a knife or fork: if the juices run out clear, the chicken is cooked. If using a meat thermometer, the chicken should be cooked until it reaches 165°F. Remove from the pan with tongs and set on paper towels or a rack to drain.

To make the waffles: Preheat a waffle iron according to the manufacturer's instructions. Mix together the flour, baking powder, salt, sugar, and baking soda in a large bowl. In a small bowl, whisk together the buttermilk, egg, and butter until uniform in consistency. Stir the buttermilk mixture into the flour mixture until well incorporated. Pour 1 cup of batter into the waffle iron and cook until golden.

Top the waffles with a piece of fried chicken and pour some maple syrup over them if you like. Enjoy!

HASH BROWNS

BY FELIX KYSYL

" I love hash browns because you don't have to cook them individually. You just put everything in the oven, and you're done! And being 'done' without much effort is essential on Sunday mornings. "

40 MINS ⋮ SERVES 6

INGREDIENTS

4 medium potatoes, peeled and grated

1 onion, diced

2 garlic cloves, minced

1 large egg

1 teaspoon Worcestershire sauce

1 tablespoon extra-virgin olive oil

Salt and pepper

Butter for greasing a baking sheet

Cornstarch for dusting

Preheat the oven to 350°F.

Press the potatoes and onion into a colander to get all the excess water out. Then transfer the mixture to a large bowl. Add the garlic, egg, Worcestershire sauce, olive oil, salt, and pepper and mix thoroughly.

Coat a baking sheet with a thin coat of butter, and lightly sprinkle the cornstarch on top so that it sticks to the butter. Only use enough cornstarch to just barely cover the butter. Spread out the potato mixture evenly on the baking sheet.

Bake for about 20 minutes, or until the mixture is set. Finish by putting under the broiler (on a low setting) for 3 to 5 minutes, or until the top is golden brown. Be careful not to burn under the broiler!

Now cut into squares and serve them up—hash browns always go well with eggs, bacon, and a little ketchup.

HUEVOS RANCHEROS

BY IULIANA CAREY

"A great way to start the day — this recipe is simple and tastes great."

(fresh salsa in the summer, store-bought salsa in the winter)

15 MINS · SERVES 4

INGREDIENTS

1 (15-ounce) can refried or whole black beans, drained

½ teaspoon vegetable oil (optional; see Quick Tips)

4 flour tortillas, 6 to 7 inches in diameter (see Quick Tips)

1 cup Jack cheese, grated

2 teaspoons butter

4 large eggs

Salt and pepper

Salsa for garnish, homemade (page 33) or store-bought

> **QUICK TIPS** Use a griddle or frying pan that can take medium to medium-high heat without scorching—that means either cast iron or carbon steel. Do not use too much oil (or butter, if you prefer)—the best pan is one that allows you to heat the tortillas dry, so they get very crispy without being greasy at all. The key to a crispy quesadilla is less fat in the pan—too much fat will make your tortilla soggy. If you do need to use oil, use just enough to coat the bottom of your frying pan, about ½ teaspoon. ✳ You can also use corn tortillas, if you wish. These will take a bit longer to cook.

Heat the beans in a medium saucepan over low heat. Once warmed, remove from heat.

Coat a large, heavy frying pan, such as cast iron, with the oil, or use it dry. Heat a tortilla in the pan over medium-high heat until just starting to brown, about 30 seconds. Flip the tortilla and while it cooks on the second side for about 30 seconds, add 2 tablespoons of beans (spread them out quickly and evenly) and 2 tablespoons of cheese. (You need to act fast here, so the tortilla doesn't burn. If this proves too difficult, you can take the tortilla off the pan to spread the beans and sprinkle the cheese on the cooked side, and then return the tortilla to the pan to cook the second side.)

Place the cooked tortilla on a plate and repeat with the other tortillas. (You can keep them in a warm oven, if you wish, but they are fine served slightly cooled, too.)

To fry the eggs, using the same frying pan, melt the butter over medium heat. Crack all 4 eggs into the frying pan and cook for 3 to 4 minutes for runny yolks and 5 to 6 minutes for firmer eggs. Feel free to flip the eggs if you do not want them sunny-side up. Season with salt and pepper.

Place a fried egg on top of each prepared tortilla, add salsa to taste, and serve.

SEASONAL MINI FRITTATAS

These mini frittatas are the perfect breakfast for those who have a tight schedule in the mornings. Make a batch on Sunday and pop them in the refrigerator, and they'll be good all week. Mini frittatas are packed with protein to keep you full, vitamins to keep you healthy, and they're portable to keep you from running late. Make sure to swap in seasonal ingredients as the seasons change to keep this breakfast fresh, tasty, and interesting.

MAKES 10-12 FRITTATAS

SPRING MINI FRITTATAS

25 MINS

INGREDIENTS
Nonstick spray
1 tablespoon extra-virgin olive oil
½ cup green onions, white and pale green parts only, sliced
2⁄3 cup asparagus, thinly sliced
8 large eggs
½ cup whole milk
2 tablespoons fresh parsley, chopped
½ teaspoon salt
½ teaspoon pepper
4 ounces crumbled goat cheese

Preheat the oven to 375°F. Spray a 12-cup muffin tin (or two 6-cup muffin tins) with nonstick cooking spray.

Heat the olive oil in a medium frying pan over medium heat. Add the green onions and asparagus to the pan and sauté until they soften, about 4 to 5 minutes.

Meanwhile, whisk the eggs, milk, parsley, salt, and pepper in a large mixing bowl. Stir in the goat cheese and the sautéed vegetables.

Pour the mixture into the muffin tins and put in the oven. Bake until the egg mixture rises a bit and is set in the center, about 8 to 10 minutes. Wrap individually in plastic wrap and store in the refrigerator to keep fresh.

SUMMER MINI FRITTATAS

25 MINS

INGREDIENTS
Nonstick spray
1 tablespoon extra-virgin olive oil
½ cup fresh corn kernels
½ cup zucchini, chopped
8 large eggs
½ cup whole milk
¼ cup fresh basil, chopped
½ teaspoon salt
½ teaspoon pepper
½ cup grated mozzarella
½ cup cherry tomatoes, halved

Preheat the oven and prepare the muffin tins according to the instructions in the Spring Frittata recipe.

Heat the olive oil in a medium frying pan over medium heat. Add the corn and zucchini and sauté until softened, about 4 to 5 minutes.

Meanwhile, whisk the eggs, milk, basil, salt, and pepper in a large mixing bowl. Stir in the mozzarella cheese, tomatoes, and sautéed vegetables.

Pour the mixture into the muffin tins and bake as directed in the Spring Frittata recipe.

🖋 AUTUMN MINI FRITTATAS

30 MINS

INGREDIENTS

Nonstick spray
1 tablespoon extra-virgin olive oil
1 large leek, white and light green parts only,
   halved and sliced
2 cups fresh spinach
8 large eggs
½ cup whole milk
1 tablespoon fresh rosemary, chopped
½ teaspoon salt
½ teaspoon pepper
½ cup grated fontina cheese

Preheat the oven and prepare the muffin tins according to the instructions in the Spring Frittata recipe.

Heat the olive oil in a large frying pan over medium heat. Add the leeks and sauté until softened, about 4 to 5 minutes. Remove from the pan and set aside. Add the spinach to the pan and cook, stirring, until reduced in volume. Remove from the pan and coarsely chop.

Whisk the eggs, milk, rosemary, salt, and pepper in a mixing bowl. Stir in the fontina cheese and the sautéed vegetables.

Pour the mixture into the muffin tins and bake as directed in the Spring Frittata recipe.

🖋 WINTER MINI FRITTATAS

30 MINS

INGREDIENTS

Nonstick spray
1 tablespoon extra-virgin olive oil
1 medium onion, diced
1 cup cremini mushrooms, chopped
1 teaspoon fresh thyme leaves
8 large eggs
½ cup whole milk
½ teaspoon salt
½ teaspoon pepper
4 ounces crumbled goat cheese

Preheat the oven and prepare the muffin tins according to the instructions in the Spring Frittata recipe.

Heat the olive oil in a medium frying pan over medium heat. Add the onion, mushrooms, and thyme and sauté until they soften, about 8 to 10 minutes.

Whisk the eggs, milk, salt, and pepper in a large mixing bowl. Stir in the goat cheese and the sautéed vegetables.

Pour the mixture into the muffin tins and bake as directed in the Spring Frittata recipe.

SOUPS, SALADS & SANDWICHES

STUFFED MUSHROOMS

BY KIM SIMPSON

"I love cooking stuffed mushrooms because they don't require too much prepara-tion. They are a good way to use up any old vegetables you have lying around, and they're great on their own for lunch or a snack, or on the side with dinner."

30 MINS : SERVES 2

INGREDIENTS

2 portobello mushrooms

Olive oil

1 tablespoon butter

6 button mushrooms, diced

2 garlic cloves, minced

½ zucchini, diced

½ red bell pepper, diced

½ onion, diced

¼ eggplant, diced

2 slices of smoked bacon, chopped (optional)

1 teaspoon salt

½ teaspoon pepper

2 tablespoons leafy fresh herbs, minced, like basil
   or parsley

½ cup diced canned tomatoes

¼ cup old-fashioned rolled oats (not instant)

2 tablespoons heavy cream (optional)

½ cup grated cheese, like mozzarella or fontina

Preheat the oven to 350°F.

Remove the stems of the portobello mushrooms and rinse the caps. Rub with olive oil and place on a baking sheet with the tops facing down.

Melt the butter in a frying pan over medium-high heat. Add the button mushrooms, garlic, zucchini, red pepper, onion, and eggplant and stir. Add the bacon. Season with salt, pepper, and fresh herbs and cook for 5 to 7 minutes, or until the vegetables are tender.

Add the tomatoes, oats, and heavy cream, if desired. Cook, stirring, until everything is cooked through and well blended. Spoon the mixture into the porto-bello mushroom caps and top with cheese. Bake for 10 minutes, or until the mushrooms have softened and the cheese has melted.

QUICK TIP Any filling that's left over is great on toast or liquefied for soup.

GREEN SALAD

BY SARAH VENIARD

"This is the ultimate summertime treat. For seasonal greens, fresh from the garden is best, so get growing in your garden or window box!"

(using seasonal greens)

15 MINS : SERVES 4

INGREDIENTS

2 to 3 small heads of seasonal greens such as chard, arugula, mizuna, or sorrel

1 (15-ounce) can flageolet beans, drained

¼ pound feta cheese

½ cup toasted seeds, such as sesame, sunflower, or flax

2 tablespoons extra-virgin olive oil

2 tablespoons balsamic vinegar

Juice of 1 lemon

1 teaspoon Dijon mustard

1 teaspoon salt

½ teaspoon pepper

Wash and dry the greens and place them in a large salad bowl. Gently mix in the beans.

Crumble the feta cheese into the bowl. Sprinkle the toasted seeds over the salad.

In a small bowl, whisk together the olive oil, balsamic vinegar, lemon juice, mustard, salt, and pepper.

Toss the dressing and the salad together.

CAESAR SALAD

BY FRANCESCA ECCLES

"Caesar Salad is a delicious meal that you can prepare whenever! The dressing is homemade as well as the croutons, which make it a homey treat."

20 MINS : SERVES 3–4

INGREDIENTS

For the Croutons

2 cups stale bread, cubed
¼ cup extra-virgin olive oil
2 teaspoons garlic powder
Salt and pepper

For the Salad

Juice of 1 lemon
2½ tablespoons mayonnaise
2 garlic cloves, minced
¼ teaspoon Dijon mustard

4½ tablespoons extra-virgin olive oil
Salt and pepper
6 to 8 cups chopped romaine lettuce
⅓ cup grated Parmesan cheese

To make the croutons: Preheat the oven to 350°F. In a large bowl, toss the cubed bread, olive oil, and garlic powder. Taste and season with salt and pepper. Spread the bread on a baking sheet and bake until golden, about 10 minutes, giving them a toss about halfway through.

To make the salad: In a medium bowl, whisk together the lemon juice, mayonnaise, garlic, and mustard. Slowly add the olive oil while whisking. Taste and season with salt and pepper. Put the romaine in a large bowl and toss with the dressing. Add the croutons and Parmesan cheese and toss again.

> **QUICK TIP** If you want to impress guests, serve this as a fancy hors d'oeuvre. Make the croutons and mix them together with the lemon juice, garlic, mustard, olive oil, salt, and pepper. Use only the inner romaine leaves, and leave them whole. Scoop a spoonful of the Caesar dressing and crouton mixture onto each leaf and sprinkle with Parmesan cheese. Voila! Caesar salad finger food.

SQUASH SALAD

BY ALEX MANUNZA

" The jalapeno-oil mix keeps really well, so you can always have a container of this in your drawer at work. This recipe works especially well with red mustard salad greens, but you can use any kind of salad green, it will still be really good. "

30 MINS : SERVES 1

INGREDIENTS

1 cup winter squash, cubed

1 tablespoon extra-virgin olive oil

2 slices prosciutto, chopped

2 cups red mustard salad leaves

1 jalapeño chile, chopped

Salt and pepper

1 slice crusty bread

Preheat the oven to 400°F.

Toss the squash with 1½ teaspoons of the olive oil and spread out on a baking sheet. Bake until cooked through and you can pierce the pieces easily with a fork. Let cool.

Toss the squash, prosciutto, and mustard leaves in a serving bowl. Mix the remaining 1½ teaspoons of olive oil and the jalapeño in a small bowl; season with salt and pepper. Dress the salad with the oil mixture.

Enjoy with crusty bread!

TUNA SALAD

BY NAOMI MINER

"This tuna Salad is super easy and pretty fast to make. It's great on its own, or served on slices of baguette or on salad greens."

 10 MINS : SERVES 2–3

INGREDIENTS

1 (10-ounce) can chunk light tuna (in water)

½ cup cherry tomatoes, halved

⅓ cup of your favorite olives, chopped

2 teaspoons mayonnaise

1 teaspoon Dijon mustard

Salt and pepper

Sliced baguette for serving

1 tablespoon chopped fresh herbs, such as parsley or basil

Stir together the tuna, tomatoes, olives, mayonnaise, and mustard in a medium bowl. Taste and season with salt and pepper.

Spread on bread slices and top with the fresh herbs.

QUICK TIPS To serve this as a salad, toss about 4 cups of seasonal greens with vinaigrette (page 31) and top with the tuna and fresh herbs. ❋ Use homemade mayonnaise instead of store bought for best results (page 33). And if mayonnaise just isn't your thing, omit it, and substitute tuna canned in olive oil instead of water.

FLOWER PRAWN SOUP

BY EMMA OGOE

"I call this dish 'Flower Prawn Soup' because the prawns bloom like little flowers when they cook. It tastes amazing!"

30 MINS : SERVES 4

INGREDIENTS

1 pound fresh king prawns (jumbo shrimp), peeled
   and deveined

4 cups water

1 tomato, chopped

1 onion, chopped

1 garlic clove, minced

1 stalk lemongrass, sliced (tender part only)

1 small jalapeño chile, chopped (optional)

½ cup frozen peas

½ cup mushrooms, sliced

4 packets shrimp-flavored instant noodles

Salt and pepper

Cut an incision lengthwise down the inside center of each prawn. When they cook, they will open up like blooming flowers. Set aside.

Bring the water to a boil. Add the tomato, onion, garlic, and lemongrass. If you prefer a spicier soup, add the jalapeño. Bring to a boil and continue boiling for 2 to 3 minutes.

Add the peas and mushrooms, and boil for another 3 minutes. Add the shrimp-flavored noodles and stir until softened. Add the prawns and continue to cook until they turn pink and are cooked through, about 3 minutes.

To serve, use tongs to pull out the noodles and divide among four soup bowls. Ladle the broth, prawns, and vegetables over the noodles in each bowl. Salt and pepper to taste.

CHICKEN NOODLE SOUP WITH CHEESE MUFFINS

BY ROSCOE SAVAGE

" This is great if you need quick comfort food. If you are in a real hurry, you can leave out some of the seasoning and use a packet of chicken-flavored noodles! The bits in the cheese muffins can be any leftover ingredients. A great recipe for using up what you find in the fridge."

50 MINS : MAKES 4 SERVINGS OF SOUP AND 12 MUFFINS

INGREDIENTS

For the Soup

4½ cups chicken stock, homemade (page 34) or
    store-bought
3 boneless, skinless chicken breast halves, cut into
    thin strips
2 packages plain ramen noodles
3 green onions, thinly sliced
2 to 3 Little Gem or Butter lettuce leaves, sliced
½ cup frozen peas
⅓ cup green beans, sliced
2 teaspoons soy sauce
2 teaspoons hoisin sauce
Salt and pepper

For the Muffins

1 cup self-rising flour
½ cup milk
⅓ cup polenta
2 large eggs
2 tablespoons grated cheddar or mozzarella cheese
1 tablespoon sugar
4 spring onions, chopped
3 slices bacon, cooked and crumbled
½ cup canned creamed sweet corn
1 (2-ounce) block cheddar cheese

To make the soup: Bring the chicken stock to a boil in a soup pot, and keep it boiling for 6 minutes. Add the chicken, reduce the heat, and simmer for 5 minutes. Add the remaining ingredients and simmer until the noodles are cooked through. When the muffins are ready, pour into individual bowls, sprinkle with salt and pepper, and serve with spoons and chopsticks, accompanied by the muffins.

To make the muffins: Preheat the oven to 350°F. Grease a 12-cup muffin tin or line with paper liners. Stir together the flour, milk, polenta, eggs, grated cheese, and sugar in a large mixing bowl until blended into a smooth batter. Fold in the spring onions, bacon, and corn. Spoon the batter into the prepared muffin tin.

Cut the block of cheddar cheese into 12 equal cubes; push one cheese cube into each muffin. Bake for 20 minutes, or until a toothpick comes out clean when pierced through the muffin. Serve warm.

SARAH'S RAMEN

BY SARAH DUVELIER

"This soup is inspired by one of my favorite Japanese dishes: ramen! I wanted to offer a new twist on the classic recipe, and even if it's not an original Japanese creation, it tastes delicious and it's really easy to make!"

30 MINS : SERVES 4

INGREDIENTS

1 to 2 tablespoons sesame oil

1 (14-ounce) package firm tofu, drained and cut into
    1-inch cubes

1 tablespoon sesame seeds

½ cup plus 1 tablespoon soy sauce

½ pound portobello mushrooms, sliced

⅓ pound sugar snap peas

½ pound asparagus, chopped

¼ cup miso paste

2 tablespoons grated peeled ginger

Salt and pepper

⅔ pound rice noodles

½ cup bean sprouts

2 green onions, white and light green parts only, sliced

Coat the bottom of a large frying pan with sesame oil. Heat the oil over medium heat. Add the tofu and sear on all sides. Sprinkle with the sesame seeds and add the ½ cup of soy sauce. Cook for 2 to 3 more minutes, flipping to prevent burning. Set aside.

Bring a large saucepan of water to a boil. Add the mushrooms and sugar snap peas, and cook for 5 minutes. Add the asparagus and cook for 6 minutes more.

Add the miso paste and stir until it dissolves. Add the ginger and remaining 1 tablespoon of soy sauce. Taste and season with salt and pepper. Add the rice noodles and cook, stirring, for 2 minutes. Add the bean sprouts and remove from the heat.

Divide the soup among four soup bowls. Top with the seared tofu and green onions.

It's ready!

HEALTHY BURGERS WITH A KICK

BY JOCELYN BONO

"There's nothing like a good burger right off the grill, and 'firing up the barbie' for my family and friends is one of my favorite things to do!"

30 MINS | SERVES 4

INGREDIENTS

½ pound jalapeño chiles, halved and seeded
½ cup breadcrumbs
3 tablespoons low-fat milk
1 tablespoon fresh cilantro, chopped
½ teaspoon ground cumin
½ teaspoon paprika
½ teaspoon salt
¼ teaspoon pepper
1 pound ground turkey breast
4 whole-wheat buns
1 avocado, sliced (when in season)
Romaine leaves for serving
Tomato slices for serving (when in season)

Place the jalapeños on a grill over medium heat. Cook for about 5 minutes on each side. Let cool and dice. Set aside.

Mix together the breadcrumbs, milk, cilantro, cumin, paprika, salt, and pepper in a medium bowl. Put the ground turkey and jalapeños in a large bowl. Fold in the breadcrumb mixture. Form into four equal patties. Grill until cooked through, flipping once, about 8 minutes per side (see Quick Tips).

To toast the buns, split the bun open, place cut-side down on the grill, and grill until light golden brown, about 10 seconds.

Place the patties on the buns and top each burger with a quarter of the avocado. Top with romaine leaves and tomatoes slices, if desired.

QUICK TIPS You may have to oil the grill grate so the patties don't stick. To do this, moisten a paper towel with a little oil and rub it on the grate. ✳ Instead of the usual French fries, serve with a healthier side dish! Serve with Fava Beans (page 72) in the spring, grilled ears of corn or bell peppers in the summer, brussels-sprout hash in the fall, or roasted squash in the winter. You can substitute 1½ teaspoons crushed red pepper for the peppers and hummus for the avocado if you are making the burgers in the winter.

SAUSAGE BOLOGNESE

BY JANEK FLEMYNG

" This recipe is very easy and very cheap. It doesn't take long to make and reminds me of family meals. It's also great before a night out. "

 1.25 HRS : SERVES 4

INGREDIENTS

1 to 2 tablespoons extra-virgin olive oil

2 large white onions, diced

3 garlic cloves, minced

1 red bell pepper, diced

6 to 8 mild Italian sausages, cut into 4 to 5 pieces each

2 carrots, peeled and chopped

1 (15-ounce) can chopped tomatoes

1 cup stock, such as pork or chicken

1 teaspoon dried oregano

1 pound rigatoni

1 tablespoon crème fraîche

1 tablespoon butter

½ cup fresh parsley, roughly chopped

1 tablespoon fresh lemon juice

Grated Parmesan cheese for garnish

Coat a large soup pot with olive oil. Heat the oil over medium-low heat and add the onions, garlic, and red pepper; stir until softened. Add the sausages and carrots and cook for 7 minutes, or until the sausage is browned.

Add the tomatoes, stock, and oregano and bring to a boil. Reduce the heat and simmer for 30 minutes, or until the sauce has reduced by a quarter.

Meanwhile, bring a large pot of salted water to a boil. Add the pasta and cook according to the package instructions until al dente (firm but tender). Drain the pasta and add to the sausage pot.

Stir the crème fraîche and butter into the sauce. Add the parsley and lemon juice.

Ladle the stew into individual serving bowls. Top with Parmesan cheese.

> QUICK TIPS If you prefer a spicier Bolognese, swap out the mild Italian sausage for spicy Italian, or add a tablespoon of chopped jalapeños (or a teaspoon of crushed red pepper flakes) when adding the red peppers. ※ And if you're not in the mood for pasta, serve the Bolognese in individual serving bowls with thick slices of Italian bread for dipping. Make sure there's enough bread to mop up all of the delicious sauce!

SEASONAL SANDWICHES

It's easy to get stuck eating the same ol' boring sandwiches over and over again. Keep it interesting by creating seasonal and fresh sandwiches. Be adventurous and try different varieties of bread, spreads and jams, meats, cheeses, fruits, and veggies. You never know what your next favorite sandwich might be.

MAKES 1 SANDWICH

❄ SPRING EGG SALAD SANDWICH

10 MINS

INGREDIENTS

5 asparagus spears, sliced

1 tablespoon balsamic vinegar

1½ teaspoons mayonnaise

1 teaspoon Dijon mustard

1 teaspoon fresh lemon juice

2 teaspoons chopped fresh parsley

2 hard-boiled eggs, chopped (see Quick Tips)

2 slices whole-wheat bread, lightly toasted

1 slice Swiss cheese (optional)

Preheat the broiler.

Toss the asparagus and vinegar together in a bowl. Spread out the asparagus on a baking sheet and broil until tender, turning once, about 5 to 7 minutes.

Mix the mayonnaise, Dijon mustard, lemon juice, and parsley in a medium bowl. Stir in the asparagus. Gently fold in the egg.

Spoon the mixture over one slice of bread, top with the Swiss cheese, if desired, and the second piece of bread.

> QUICK TIPS   For a perfect hard boiled egg, bring a pot of water (enough to cover your eggs) to a boil, then bring down to a simmer. Add your eggs and cook for 9 to 10 minutes. Put the eggs in cold water to stop them from cooking. Peel when completely cool. ❄ For a healthier sandwich, use only boiled egg whites. Use the egg yolks to make homemade Mayonnaise (page 33), which is much healthier and tastier than store-bought mayonnaise .

❄ SUMMER CRUNCHY VEGGIE SANDWICH

10 MINS

INGREDIENTS

1 to 2 ounces soft goat cheese

1 teaspoon fresh lemon juice

1 tablespoon chopped fresh leafy herbs

2 slices whole-wheat bread, lightly toasted

¼ cucumber, peeled and sliced

4 radishes, sliced

1 carrot, peeled and grated

⅓ cup watercress, chopped

2 to 3 ounces smoked salmon (optional)

In a small bowl, mix the goat cheese, lemon juice, and fresh herbs. Spread evenly on both bread slices. Pile the remaining ingredients on one slice of bread, and top with the other slice.

EARLY AUTUMN FIG AND PROSCIUTTO SANDWICH

10 MINS

INGREDIENTS

1 tablespoon Pesto (page 32)

1 small ciabatta roll, sliced for a sandwich

1 to 2 ounces Brie cheese

3 slices prosciutto

2 fresh figs, thinly sliced

½ cup leafy autumn greens, such as arugula, chard, or kale

Spread the pesto evenly on one cut side of the roll. Spread the Brie evenly on the other cut side. Fill with prosciutto, figs, and leafy greens.

QUICK TIP Feel free to get versatile with this sandwich! Use chimichurri sauce (page 98) instead of pesto. Or, sub-stitute your favorite cured ham—such as Serrano ham or salami—for the prosciutto.

WINTER SQUASH GRILLED CHEESE

55 MINS

INGREDIENTS

¼ butternut squash, cut in ¼-inch-thick slices

1 teaspoon extra-virgin olive oil

1 teaspoon salt

½ teaspoon pepper

1½ teaspoons butter, plus more as needed

¼ onion, sliced and separated into rings

1 tablespoon balsamic vinegar

1½ teaspoons chopped fresh sage

1 to 2 ounces fresh mozzarella, cut into 2 slices

2 slices sourdough bread

Preheat the oven to 400°F.

Toss the squash with olive oil, salt, and pepper, and spread on a baking sheet. Bake for about 35 to 40 minutes, or until the slices are cooked through.

Meanwhile, melt the butter in a medium frying pan over medium heat. Add the onion and cook for 15 minutes, stirring occasionally, until softened. Stir in the balsamic vinegar and sage and continue cooking for another 10 minutes, or until the onions are golden in color.

Spread butter on one side of each piece of bread. Put one slice of bread, butter-side down, on another medium frying pan over medium heat. Top with, in this order, a slice of mozzarella, the squash, onions, and the remaining slice of mozzarella. Top with the other slice of bread, butter-side up. Cook until the cheese is melted and the bread is browned, about 3 minutes on each side.

Chapter

5

· · · · · · · · · · · · ·

SNACKS & SIDES

HUMMUS

BY ERIC PRADEUX

"This is so easy to do! My mom showed me how to make it once, and now I want it all the time! It's a good snack, and it's better when you do it yourself, rather than buy it from a store!"

 10 MINS ⋮ MAKES 2½ CUPS

INGREDIENTS

1 (15-ounce) can chickpeas, drained

2 teaspoons extra-virgin olive oil

2 teaspoons fresh lemon juice

2 garlic cloves, crushed

1 tablespoon tahini (optional)

½ teaspoon paprika

½ teaspoon ground cumin

Salt and pepper

Add the chickpeas, olive oil, lemon juice, garlic, and tahini, if desired, to a blender or food processor. Blend until smooth. Stir in the paprika and cumin. Taste, and season with salt and pepper. Keep in the fridge (it will last up to 7 days), and serve cool on warm pita bread or toast.

> **QUICK TIPS** Chickpeas aren't your favorite? Feel free to swap them for your preferred variety of creamy white beans: try cannellini beans, great northern beans, or butter beans, for example. ※ Try adding toppings to keep your hummus festive. Once you've finished making the recipe, top with chopped roasted bell peppers, chopped olives, roasted garlic, or any leftover fresh herbs that you have in the fridge.

GUACAMOLE

BY GABRIEL DE VILLAINES

"My cousin Alix came back from Mexico after spending a year in the capital city. She's the one who taught me how to make guacamole. Since then, I've been making it every time people come to our house – and everybody loves it!"

10 MINS ⋮ MAKES ¾ CUP

INGREDIENTS

1 ripe avocado

1 tomato, diced

1 onion, diced

Juice of 1 lime

1 teaspoon salt

½ teaspoon pepper

½ teaspoon paprika

2 drops Tabasco

Mash the avocado with a fork in a medium bowl. Fold in the tomato and onion. Sprinkle with lime juice, salt, pepper, paprika, and Tabasco. Gently stir until everything is incorporated.

It's ready! And it's delicious with tortilla chips.

QUICK TIPS The best way to tell if an avocado is ready to use is to check out the mark where the stem was removed: If it is green, the avocado is ripe; if it is brown, the avocado is overripe. ✳ To ripen an avocado, put it in a brown paper bag and store in a dark place at room temperature for a few days. ✳ To help prevent avocados from browning, sprinkle the peeled avocado with a bit of lemon juice.

FAVA BEANS

BY PAUL HANNAGEN

"This is an easy recipe. However, with all easy recipes the secret lies in the execution both of cooking and seasoning."

 15 MINS : MAKES 2½ CUPS

INGREDIENTS

2 cups whole fava beans

3 tablespoons butter

¼ pound pancetta (smoked pork belly) or thick-cut bacon, sliced

2 teaspoons extra-virgin olive oil

1 teaspoon Chardonnay vinegar

Salt and pepper

Bring a large pan of salted water to a boil. Add the beans to the boiling water, and cook for 4 minutes. Drain the beans, and add them to a bowl of ice cold water. Once the beans have cooled, gently remove them from their pods.

In a large frying pan, melt the butter over medium-high heat. Add the pancetta and cook, stirring continuously, for 3 to 5 minutes, until cooked through. Take care not to burn the butter. Remove the pancetta and set aside.

Increase the heat to high and add the beans to the frying pan. Cook, stirring constantly, until the beans are warmed through, 1 to 2 minutes.

Combine the beans with the pancetta, olive oil, and vinegar in a mixing bowl. Taste and season with salt and pepper.

Transfer to a small dish and serve.

QUICK TIP   For best results, add enough salt to the water so that it tastes a little like seawater.

VEGETABLE COUSCOUS

BY SAM WELL

"Couscous is pretty bland and unexciting on its own, but it works like a flavor sponge. All you need to do is give it a load of big exciting ingredients for it to soak up, and then sit back and watch it transform into something fantastic!"

50 MINS : SERVES 8

INGREDIENTS

2 red onions, chopped

2 red or yellow bell peppers, chopped

1 large zucchini, chopped

4 medium tomatoes, chopped

¼ cup fresh parsley, chopped

4 garlic cloves, minced

2 tablespoons extra-virgin olive oil

1 tablespoon balsamic vinegar

Salt and pepper

⅓ cup your favorite olives, chopped

⅓ cup artichoke hearts, chopped

Juice of 1 lemon

2 cups couscous

¾ cup crumbled feta cheese

Preheat the oven to 400°F. Bring a medium pot of water to a boil.

Toss the onions, peppers, zucchini, tomatoes, parsley, and garlic with the oil and vinegar and spread out in a large roasting pan. Sprinkle with salt and pepper. Roast in the oven for 25 to 30 minutes, giving the vegetables a stir halfway through.

In a large mixing bowl, toss the olives and artichokes with the lemon juice. Once the vegetables have finished roasting, add them to the bowl. Add the couscous and stir the mixture together. Add enough boiling water to cover the vegetable couscous, and let sit. After 5 minutes, check the mixture. If there's still water, stir until absorbed. If it's dry, add a bit more water and let sit for another minute.

When the couscous is as desired, top with feta cheese.

QUICK TIP Serve the couscous with some lettuce tossed in a very light dressing, like a vinaigrette (see page 31).

VEGETABLE TOAST

BY JEREMY LICKERY

"This is the easiest way to trick people into thinking you can make appetizers, and it's also a tasty, cheesy snack."

25 MINS : SERVES 4

INGREDIENTS

4 plain English muffins

1 zucchini, julienned (cut into matchsticks)

3 teaspoons extra-virgin olive oil

1 garlic clove, minced

1 (15-ounce) can crushed tomatoes

1 (15-ounce) can tomato purée

4 tablespoons soft goat cheese

2 tablespoons chopped fresh basil

Preheat the broiler.

Cut each muffin in half and lightly toast. (Two halves per person is good for a snack or appetizer.)

Spread out the zucchini on a baking sheet, drizzle with 2 teaspoons of the olive oil, and place under the broiler until tender. (Leave the broiler turned on!)

Heat the remaining teaspoon of olive oil in a medium saucepan over medium heat. Add the garlic and sauté until fragrant. Add the crushed tomatoes and simmer until slightly reduced, about 10 minutes. Add the tomato purée, stir and simmer until everything is incorporated.

Once the sauce has thickened, spread it on the muffins. Top with the goat cheese and zucchini. Transfer to a clean baking sheet and place under the broiler until the goat cheese just starts to brown and melt. Sprinkle with basil and serve.

MARINATED PEPPERS BRUSCHETTA

BY HELLY KAGE

"Lovely recipe, for lovely times! It's simple but impressive. It's good, but healthy. My friends always love it when I make some, and the peppers also remind me of snails for some reason!"

3 HRS : SERVES 2

INGREDIENTS

2 bell peppers in different colors, such as red and yellow
2 garlic cloves, crushed
3 tablespoons extra-virgin olive oil
2 tablespoons chopped fresh parsley
½ teaspoon salt
¼ teaspoon pepper

Preheat the oven to 350°F.

Put the peppers on a baking sheet and roast in the oven until their skins brown, turning occasionally, about 30 to 40 minutes. Remove from the oven and let them cool. Skin the peppers, remove the seeds, and cut the peppers into thin slices.

Mix the remaining ingredients in a container large enough to hold the peppers. Add the peppers and mix well. If the peppers aren't coated in the olive oil, add a bit more. Cover and refrigerate for at least 2 hours.

Serve with warm toasted bread.

PESTO CHERRY TOMATO PIE

BY SHAZ BLOGGS

"This is a very yummy recipe, but it's only dairy free if you make the pesto yourself, without Parmesan, which I usually do – still tastes great!"

2.5 HRS | SERVES 4

INGREDIENTS

For the Dough

½ cup rice flour, plus more for dusting

½ cup corn flour

1 teaspoon salt

¼ teaspoon baking powder

2 large eggs

1½ teaspoon extra-virgin olive oil

Pie weights or dried beans

For the Filling

¼ cup Pesto (page 32), made without cheese

2 cups halved cherry tomatoes

3 large eggs

2 tablespoons soy cream

½ teaspoon salt

¼ teaspoon pepper

1 teaspoon ground nutmeg

Grated dairy-free cheese for sprinkling (optional)

To make the dough: Mix the rice flour, corn flour, salt, and baking powder in a large bowl. Stir in the eggs and olive oil. Slowly add water, 1 tablespoon at a time—enough so that you can just form a ball without the dough sticking to your fingers. Wrap the ball in plastic wrap, and put in the fridge for 1 hour.

Preheat the oven to 400°F. Roll out the dough on parchment paper lightly dusted with flour, and then transfer the dough to a pie dish. Poke holes into the pastry shell with a fork. Put a second sheet of parchment paper over the pastry shell, and top with pie weights or dried beans. Bake for 30 to 40 minutes. Remove from the oven. Remove the pie weights and parchment paper and let cool.

To make the filling: Spread the pesto all over the cooked pastry. Put the cherry tomatoes on top of the pesto. Whisk the eggs in a medium bowl and add the cream, salt, pepper, and nutmeg. Pour over the tomatoes and sprinkle with grated cheese, if desired. Bake for 30 minutes, or until the pie shell is golden.

SCALLION PANCAKES

BY EMILY LIU

"We eat these all year long: at home or in restaurants, on regular weekdays or for special occasions. They're delicious!"

1.5 HRS | SERVES 4–5

INGREDIENTS

2 cups all-purpose flour

½ teaspoon salt, plus more for pancakes

1 bunch green onions, dark green part only, sliced

⅔ cup boiling water and ⅓ cup cold water

¼ cup vegetable oil, plus more for frying

In a large bowl, combine the flour and ½ teaspoon of salt. Add three-quarters of the scallions and mix. Stir in the ⅔ cup boiling water, and blend well. Add the ⅓ cup cold water, stirring until well mixed. Cover with a damp cloth and set aside for 10 minutes.

Knead the dough. If it becomes sticky, add a bit more flour.

Separate the dough into even balls; the number will depend on how many pancakes you want to make. On a lightly floured surface, use a rolling pin to roll out each ball into a flat disc. Top each one with cooking oil, ½ teaspoon at a time. Use your fingers to spread the oil so it covers the dough in a thin layer. When finished, sprinkle the discs with a pinch of salt and the remaining scallions.

Next, roll up each disc so it is in the form of a cylinder. Then coil the dough, so it looks like a tightly wound spring. Flatten with the rolling pin, turn it over, and let sit for another 30 minutes.

Roll each dough piece into a flattened disc again. (If you do not want to eat right away, store the dough in the freezer at this time.) Coat a large frying pan with vegetable oil over medium heat. Add the discs and cook until golden brown, about 2 to 3 minutes on each side. Be sure to keep the discs moving so that they don't stick to the pan. Cook the pancakes in batches if necessary to avoid overcrowding the pan.

Enjoy!

MINI PIZZAS

BY FELIX LOUIS BERTRAND

" These mini pizzas are perfect when you have friends over because they are really easy and quick to make. When you make a big pizza and have some dough left over, it's also a good way to use it."

30 MINS : MAKES 4–6 PIZZAS

INGREDIENTS

½ cup all-purpose flour

½ teaspoon salt

¼ teaspoon baking powder

1 large egg

2 tablespoons extra-virgin olive oil

1 (15-ounce) can tomato purée

¼ cup ground almonds

2 tablespoons balsamic vinegar

Salt and pepper

1 tomato, chopped (when in season)

Pumpkin seeds for sprinkling (optional)

Fresh or dried rosemary (optional)

Preheat the oven to 325°F.

Mix the flour, salt, and baking powder in a large bowl. Whisk in the egg and oil. Slowly drizzle in enough water so that you can just form a ball, but not so much that the dough sticks to your fingers.

Make four to six small balls out of the dough and flatten them with your fingers. Shape them like small pizzas and place them on a parchment-lined baking sheet.

In a bowl, mix the tomato purée, ground almonds, balsamic vinegar, salt, and pepper. There are no right or wrong quantities. It's all about the way you want it to taste, so just make sure you make a thick paste.

Spread the mixture on your pizzas and add chopped tomato. If you'd like, finish off with pumpkin seeds and rosemary. Put the pizzas in the oven and bake for 5 to 10 minutes, or until lightly browned and bubbling.

SPANISH TORTILLA

BY MIKE SILVER JUNIOR

"This is a classic recipe that is so simple, despite the list of ingredients. Change the filling to whatever you want, by all means. The only thing that must remain constant is the ratio of egg, onion, and potato – the rest is up to you!"

1.25 HRS : SERVES 6–8

INGREDIENTS

2 tablespoons extra-virgin olive oil, divided, plus more for drizzling

2 medium onions, thinly sliced

Salt and pepper

2 large potatoes, peeled and sliced into rounds

3 Spanish chorizo links, diced

10 large eggs

2 tomatoes, sliced

2 roasted red peppers, cut into strips

1 tablespoon basil, chopped

Preheat the oven to 350°F.

Heat 1 tablespoon of olive oil in a large frying pan over medium heat. Add the onions and season with salt and pepper. Cook, stirring occasionally, for about 5 minutes. Decrease the heat to low, and cook the onions until golden brown and cooked through. Remove from the pan and set aside. Wipe out the pan.

Meanwhile, line a baking sheet with the potatoes and drizzle with olive oil. Roast in the oven until golden brown, but not crisp, about 20 to 25 minutes. Set the potatoes aside and leave the oven on.

Place the large frying pan over high heat. Add the chorizo and cook until lightly colored. Set aside.

Beat the eggs in a large bowl and season with salt and pepper. Add the onions, potatoes, chorizo, tomatoes, roasted peppers, and basil. Pour into a casserole dish and bake for 15 to 20 minutes, or until the eggs are set. Rotate halfway through to ensure even cooking.

FRIED TOFU WITH PEANUT DIPPING SAUCE

BY JACK COUSINEAU

"Tofu, also known as bean curd, is a pretty magical ingredient. A staple in Asia for more than 2,000 years, there are countless ways to prepare it. Combine cooked tofu with your favorite sauce, and you have a tasty, high-protein meal."

40 MINS : SERVES 6

INGREDIENTS

For the Tofu

1 (14-ounce) package firm organic (refrigerated) tofu

½ cup grape seed, canola, or other vegetable oil

For the Sauce

1/3 cup unsweetened, organic peanut butter

½ cup of very hot water

1 teaspoon soy sauce

1 teaspoon brown sugar

1 teaspoon fish sauce (optional)

¼ clove garlic, minced and sautéed (optional)

Pinch of your favorite hot chili sauce or dried hot pepper flakes (optional)

Pinch of grated ginger (optional)

To prepare the tofu: Remove from the packaging and drain the liquid. Cut the tofu into 1-inch slices and then cut the slices into your favorite shape—triangles, cubes, or rectangles are perfect for dipping.

Place a clean towel on a baking sheet. Place the tofu shapes in a single layer on top of the towel and cover with another towel and top that with a cutting board. Place something heavy on the cutting board so the tofu is gently pressed down (the cloth will soak up any extra liquid, allowing for a more crunchy fried tofu). While the tofu is draining, prepare the peanut sauce.

To make the sauce: Add all of the ingredients for the peanut dipping sauce into a blender. Blend well at medium speed. Add optional ingredients to taste (tastes great if you add them all!). If the blended sauce is too thick, add an extra teaspoon or two of very hot water. If it's too thin, add a tiny bit more peanut butter. When the sauce is blended to a consistency and taste to your liking, spoon it into a small serving bowl.

To make the tofu: Heat the oil in a large frying pan over medium-high heat (the oil should be ½ to ¾ inch deep). When the oil is hot, reduce the heat slightly and place the tofu slices in the pan with tongs. Cook until golden brown, about 2 minutes, then turn and repeat on the other side. Place the fried tofu on a clean paper towel to drain off excess oil. Serve the tofu on a plate with the bowl of peanut dipping sauce on the side.

OAXACAN SQUASH BLOSSOM QUESADILLA WITH CHIPOTLE CREMA

BY DANIEL MENDELSON

" I got inspired by Mexican cooking when I went on a vacation to Oaxaca. The flavor of the squash blossoms is subtle, but the chipotle crema gives it a pretty good kick. "

25 MINS | SERVES 4

INGREDIENTS

For the Chipotle Crema

1 cup Mexican crema, sour cream, or crème fraîche

1 (7-ounce) can of chipotle peppers in adobo sauce

For the Quesadilla

½ teaspoon butter or vegetable oil, if using
 (see Quick Tips)

¼ pound Mexican (uncooked) chorizo, casings removed

4 flour tortillas (6 to 7 inches in diameter)

2 cups grated Monterey Jack or cheddar cheese

8 squash blossoms, stemmed (see Quick Tips)

1 red onion, thinly sliced

1 small tomato, thinly sliced

Cilantro sprigs for garnish

QUICK TIPS   Use a griddle or frying pan that can take medium to medium-high heat without scorching—that means either cast-iron or carbon steel. Do not use too much butter or oil—the best pan is one that allows you to heat the tortillas dry, so they get very crispy without being greasy at all. The key to a crispy quesadilla is less fat in the pan—too much fat will make your tortilla soggy. If you do need to use butter or oil, use just enough to coat the bottom of your frying pan, about ½ teaspoon. ※ You can buy squash blossoms at specialty food stores and farmers' markets throughout the summer. To prepare them, gently open the petals and inspect them for insects. Wash the blossoms and snap off the stems. The delicate petals may tear a bit, but don't worry, you can still use them.

To make the chipotle crema: Place the Mexican crema and 1 or 2 whole chipotle chiles (depending on how spicy you want it) in a food processor. Pulse until fully blended, about 1 minute.

To make the quesadilla: Melt the butter in a medium frying pan over medium heat. Add the chorizo. Break up the chorizo with a wooden spoon and sauté until browned, crumbly, and crisp, about 10 minutes. Set aside.

Warm a large frying pan (see Quick Tips) over medium-high heat, and heat a tortilla until just starting to brown, about 30 seconds. Flip the tortilla and sprinkle cheese on half of the browned side. Top with 2 squash blossoms, 2 slices of onion, 2 slices of tomato, and 2 tablespoons of chorizo. Fold over the tortilla and continue to cook on both sides until the tortilla is brown and crispy and the cheese has melted, about 30 seconds each side.

To serve, cut into wedges and top each one with chipotle crema and a sprig of cilantro.

SEASONAL FRUIT SALAD

While fruit salads should be enjoyed year round, as we all know, fruits are seasonal—just because watermelon is on display in your local super-market in the middle of winter doesn't mean you should buy it. If you want your fruit salad to be a hit from January to December, be sure to use only the ripest, seasonal fruits. And the closer to home they're grown, the better.

SERVES 4

❋ LATE SPRING APRICOT SALAD

10 MINS

INGREDIENTS

8 cups seasonal leafy greens

3 tablespoons crumbled goat cheese

Garlicky croutons (see page 56)

Vinaigrette Dressing (page 31) with shallots
   (see Quick Tip, page 31)

4 to 5 apricots, sliced

Toss the greens, goat cheese, and croutons with the vinaigrette in a large serving bowl. Top with the apricots and serve immediately.

> QUICK TIP   For an extra-impressive salad, halve the apri-cots, remove the pits, drizzle with balsamic vinegar, and grill, cut-side down. Feel free to use other late-spring or summer stone fruit, like peaches, nectarines, or firm plums.

❋ SUMMER BERRY SALAD

10 MINS

INGREDIENTS

½ pound strawberries, hulled and quartered

2 cups mixed summer berries, such as raspberries,
   blueberries, and blackberries

⅓ cup fresh mint leaves, roughly chopped

Juice of 1 lemon

2 teaspoons honey

Whipped cream for serving

In a large bowl, combine the strawberries, mixed berries, and mint.

In a small bowl, whisk together the lemon juice and honey. Add to the fruit bowl and toss. Separate to individual bowls, and top with whipped cream.

BAKED AUTUMN PEARS AND APPLES

55 MINS

INGREDIENTS

2 firm medium pears (with peel on), such as Anjou or
  Bosc, halved and cored
2 medium baking apples (with peel on), such as Mutsu,
  Honeycrisp, or Granny Smith, halved and cored
Juice of 1 lemon
2 tablespoons unsalted butter, cut into 8 cubes
½ cup light brown sugar
1 teaspoon ground cinnamon

Preheat the oven to 350°F.

Place the fruit halves in a casserole dish, peel-side
up. Drizzle the lemon juice over the fruit. Place 1 cube
of butter on each piece.

In a small bowl, mix together the sugar and cinnamon. Sprinkle evenly over the fruit. Cover with foil
and bake for 35 to 40 minutes, or until softened.

QUICK TIP   Peak under the foil after about 15 to 20
minutes. If the fruit looks too dry, add liquid, such as apple
juice, diluted lemon juice, or water, about ¼ cup at a time.
CAUTION! Do not add cold liquid to a hot glass dish! The
difference in temperature will cause the glass to shatter.

WINTER CITRUS SALAD

15 MINS

INGREDIENTS

2 blood oranges
1 pink grapefruit
6 to 8 cups winter salad greens, such as spinach,
  watercress, or kale
½ cup pomegranate seeds
Vinaigrette Dressing (page 31) with shallots (see Quick Tip,
  page 31) and 1 teaspoon honey instead of mustard

Peel the citrus, removing as much of the pith as possible (see Quick Tip). Cut the oranges into half wheels
and the grapefruit into quarter wheels. Set aside.

Toss the salad greens and pomegranate seeds with the
vinaigrette. Top with the citrus and serve immediately.

QUICK TIP   Removing all of the skin and pith from citrus
can be difficult. Give this method a try. Cut off the ends of
the citrus, just enough so that the fruit is visible. Going from
top to bottom, slice off the peel in 1- to 1½-inch segments,
until all of the peel is removed. Inspect the fruit, and slice
off any remaining pith. Finally, cut from the outside to the
center between the membrane and fruit of each segment.
When both sides of a segment have been separated from the
membrane, gently nudge the fruit out with the knife.

Chapter

6

. . . .

MAIN COURSES

SPANISH–STYLE BOLOGNESE

BY OLIVER QUELCH

"This recipe is a Spanish take on a Bolognese sauce, a smoky twist on a well-known classic. It's especially good as a winter warmer."

2.5 HRS : SERVES 4

INGREDIENTS

1 tablespoon extra-virgin olive oil

¼ pound Spanish chorizo, chopped

1 pound ground beef

1 red onion, chopped

1 celery stalk, chopped

1 carrot, peeled and chopped

1 garlic clove, minced

1 (28-ounce) can chopped tomatoes

2 teaspoons tomato purée

¾ cup beef stock

½ teaspoon paprika (optional)

Salt and pepper

Cooked spaghetti or tagliatelle for serving

Heat the olive oil in a large saucepan over medium-high heat. Add the chorizo and fry until crispy. Add the ground beef and fry until browned. Remove the meat from the pan by straining in a sieve and set aside. You can also use a slotted spoon.

Add the onion, celery, carrot, and garlic to the pan. Reduce the heat to low and cook, stirring occasionally, for 10 minutes, or until softened. Return the meat to the pan and add the chopped tomatoes, tomato purée, and beef stock. Add the paprika, if desired.

Bring to a boil, reduce the heat, and simmer for at least 1½ hours (the longer you cook the bolognese, the thicker it will become). Cook until you reach a desired consistency. Taste and season with salt and pepper.

Serve with spaghetti or tagliatelle.

GREEN PESTO TAGLIATELLE

BY JACK WELLS

"This dish is cheap, easy, and filling. It's my mom's recipe – and she's a pretty good chef, I have to admit."

40 MINS : SERVES 4

INGREDIENTS

1 bunch basil

2 tablespoons pine nuts

2 tablespoons grated Parmesan, Pecorino, or Grana Padano cheese

2 garlic cloves, minced

½ teaspoon salt

¼ teaspoon pepper

About 4 tablespoons extra-virgin olive oil

1 pound tagliatelle

2 slices bacon, chopped

12 button mushrooms, sliced

1 tablespoon cream

Bread for serving

Blend the basil, pine nuts, cheese, 1 clove of garlic, salt, and pepper in a food processor or blender. Slowly pour in olive oil until your pesto has reached a desired consistency. It should be wet, but not runny, like paste. Set aside.

Fill a pot with salted water and bring to a boil. Add the tagliatelle. Cook. Drain and return to the pot.

Meanwhile, heat 1 teaspoon of olive oil in a large frying pan over medium heat. Add the bacon, mushrooms, and the remaining garlic. Stir continuously until the bacon is cooked through and the mushrooms are soft. Add this mixture to the tagliatelle. Then add the cream and pesto sauce. Stir and heat through.

Serve with bread.

RISOTTO WITH ARUGULA PESTO

BY BETH GILLIAMS

"This is my father's recipe; it's one of his favorites. He taught me how to do it when I was a child, and now I keep doing it all the time because it is so simple, and at the same time so sophisticated!"

40 MINS : SERVES 2

INGREDIENTS

For the Pesto
½ cup arugula, chopped
½ garlic clove
½ cup chopped fresh basil
2 tablespoons grated Parmesan cheese
2 tablespoons extra-virgin olive oil

For the Risotto
2 cups water
1 cup chicken stock
1 tablespoon extra-virgin olive oil

½ onion, diced
½ cup risotto (Arborio) rice
⅓ cup dry white wine
2 tablespoons butter, cubed
Salt and pepper
3 tablespoons grated Parmesan cheese

To make the pesto: Put the arugula, garlic, basil, and Parmesan in a food processor or blender. Pulse a few times so everything comes together. Slowly add in the olive oil, and then a little water if necessary. The pesto should be wet, but not runny, like paste. Set aside.

To make the risotto: Heat the water and chicken stock in a saucepan until simmering and keep at a simmer. Heat the olive oil in a large frying pan over medium heat, add the onion, and stir until softened. Add the rice and cook, stirring, until the grains become transparent, about 3 minutes. Add the white wine and cook, stirring, until absorbed.

Add one ladleful of the diluted stock at a time, stirring constantly until fully absorbed. Repeat until all of the stock is added. If the rice is not at the desired consistency, continue to add simmering water, half a ladleful at a time.

Turn off the heat and stir in the butter and pesto. Season with salt and pepper. Top with grated Parmesan.

SPAGHETTI ALLA PUTTANESCA

BY SCOTT MATTOCK

"This is a cheap and easy dish to create, using mainly pantry ingredients – give it a try!"

40 MINS : SERVES 2

INGREDIENTS

½ pound spaghetti

1 (5-ounce) can tuna in oil, or ¼ cup extra-virgin olive oil

8 anchovies

1 garlic clove, thinly sliced

1 teaspoon red pepper flakes

½ cup black olives, halved

1 tablespoon capers in brine

2 tablespoons chopped fresh parsley

2 tablespoons chopped fresh basil

1 (15-ounce) can chopped tomatoes

1 lemon

Salt and pepper

Warm bread for serving

Bring a large pot of salted water to a boil. Add the spaghetti, cook according to the package directions, drain, and set aside.

If using canned tuna, pour the oil from the can into a large saucepan over medium heat (set aside the tuna). If not, add the olive oil instead. Add the anchovies to the pan and cook, stirring, until they dissolve. Add the garlic and red pepper flakes and cook, stirring, for 2 minutes.

Add the olives and the capers and stir for another minute. Add half of the fresh herbs and all of the tomatoes. Simmer over medium-low heat for about 12 minutes, until all of the flavors come together. Add the tuna at this time, if using, and simmer for another 3 minutes.

Add the remaining fresh herbs and squeeze the lemon over the sauce. Add salt and pepper to taste. Stir in the cooked spaghetti, heat it through, and serve the pasta with warm bread.

SANCOCHO

BY BRANDON JOA

"This traditional soup hails from the Dominican Republic. It's sufficient for twelve people or for a family of four for three days."

2.5 HRS | SERVES 12

INGREDIENTS

3 slices bacon (see Quick Tips)
1 whole chicken, skinned and cut into 8 pieces
   (see Quick Tips)
1 pound longaniza or other pork sausage (optional)
1 pound pork neck or ham bones
1 garlic clove, minced
1 red onion, chopped
1 large carrot, peeled and sliced ¼ inch thick
1 bunch fresh cilantro, chopped
3 ears of corn, sliced into 2-inch-thick slices
1 small pumpkin or Japanese kabocha, chopped
1 small ñame or other tuber (optional)
2 white or purple yams, chopped
1 teaspoon crushed oregano
¼ teaspoon dried basil
1½ tablespoons salt
2 plantains, chopped
1 yuca root, chopped
1 bell pepper, sliced ¼ inch thick
Beans (optional)
1 bunch collard greens, kale, or chard (optional)
Hot cooked white or brown rice for serving (optional)

Place a large stockpot (12- to 14-quart) over medium-high heat. Cook the bacon until the fat is rendered. Remove the bacon from the pot, leaving in the fat. (Save the bacon for another use. Or just eat it!)

Add the chicken, sausage, and pork bones to the pot. Cook over medium-heat, stirring occasionally, until the chicken is browned on all sides. Add the garlic and reduce the heat to medium. Add the onion, carrot, and cilantro to the pot. Cook, stirring, for 5 minutes.

Fill the pot almost all the way with water, leaving about 5 to 6 inches at the top. Increase the heat to high and add the corn and pumpkin. Bring to a boil, and then reduce the heat to medium, keeping a low boil. Add the ñame, if desired, yams, oregano, basil, and salt and cook for 30 minutes.

Reduce the heat to medium-low and add the plantains. Cook for 30 minutes. Add the yuca, bell pepper, beans, and greens, if desired. Increase the heat to high and bring to a boil. Reduce the heat to medium-low and simmer the stew for another 45 minutes, or longer if you prefer a thicker stew. Serve with rice, if desired.

Keep leftovers refrigerated and boil to reheat.

QUICK TIPS You can skip the bacon and replace the fat with 1 tablespoon of butter or olive oil. ✳ When cutting a chicken into eight pieces, you should end up with two wings, two drumsticks, two thighs, and two breasts. If butchering a chicken isn't something you're interested in doing, purchase the pieces separately from your butcher or grocery store.

CHICKEN WITH GINGER AND BROCCOLI

BY DONG TRAN

" I used to love this Vietnamese dish when my mom cooked it for me as a child. I started cooking it myself when I began living on my own. It's cheap and simple to make and can be stored in the fridge for up to 2 days."

55 MINS : SERVES 4

INGREDIENTS

4 chicken legs (thighs and drumsticks), with skin on
Salt and pepper
1 tablespoon extra-virgin olive oil
1 (2-inch) knob of ginger, peeled and diced
1 cup water
1 chicken stock cube
1 head of broccoli, chopped
Hot cooked rice for serving

Season the chicken with salt and pepper. Heat the olive oil in a large saucepan over medium-high heat. Add the chicken and the ginger. Sear the chicken on all sides.

Bring the water to a boil in a medium saucepan and dissolve the chicken stock cube in the water. Pour the stock into the pan with the chicken until just covered with liquid. Reduce the heat to low, cover, and simmer for 20 to 30 minutes. Check under the lid occasionally to be sure the liquid hasn't evaporated. If it does, add a bit more water.

When the chicken is cooked through and the sauce is reduced, add the broccoli, cover, and cook for an additional 2 to 3 minutes. Serve with rice.

CHILI CON CARNE
BY CLARE GOSLING

"This recipe is perfect when served with a big bag of plain tortilla chips and rice."

55 MINS : SERVES 4

INGREDIENTS

1 tablespoon butter
2 carrots, peeled and chopped
1 white onion, chopped
1 red onion, chopped
3 garlic cloves, minced
1 zucchini, chopped
1 green bell pepper, chopped
¾ cup cremini mushrooms, chopped
2 beef stock cubes, crushed
1 pound lean ground beef
1 (28-ounce) can plum tomatoes, with their juice
1 (15-ounce) can red kidney beans, with their liquid
1 teaspoon salt
2 teaspoons pepper
1 teaspoon hot chili powder
1 teaspoon dried basil
1 teaspoon turmeric
1 teaspoon paprika
1 bunch fresh basil, diced
1 teaspoon cornstarch
1 small bag tortilla chips
Hot cooked rice for serving

Preheat the oven to 350°F.

Melt the butter in a large pot over medium heat. Add the carrots and cook for about 4 to 5 minutes. Add the onions, garlic, zucchini, bell pepper, and mushrooms. Cook for a few minutes and add the stock cubes and ground beef. Once the vegetables start to cook through and the beef browns, add the tomatoes and the beans. Add the salt, pepper, chili powder, basil, turmeric, paprika, and ⅔ of the basil. Stir well.

Simmer the chili until the excess liquid is reduced, about 10 to 15 minutes. Add the cornstarch and stir. Transfer to a casserole dish and put in the oven. Bake for about 20 minutes.

Spoon the chili con carne into individual bowls and top with the remaining fresh basil and the tortilla chips. Serve with rice.

SUSHI

BY PAULINE BLISTENE

"I was taught how to make sushi while travelling in Japan at the age of fourteen. If you're not too picky about how traditionally made they are, sushi is a great thing to do because it impresses everyone, and it's actually pretty easy once you get used to it."

45 MINS : SERVES 8

INGREDIENTS

4 cups sushi rice, rinsed

6 cups water

2/3 cup rice vinegar

1/3 cup sugar

1 teaspoon salt

1/4 cup sesame seeds

8 seaweed sheets

1 sushi mat

3 medium carrots, peeled and julienned (cut into matchsticks)

1 cucumber, julienned

1/3 pound king prawns (jumbo shrimp), cooked

1/2 pound sushi-grade tuna, cut into strips

1/2 pound sushi-grade salmon, cut into strips

1 avocado, cut into strips

Pickled ginger for serving

Soy sauce for serving

Wasabi paste for serving

Put the rice in a large saucepan, add the water, and bring to a boil over medium heat. Add the rice and bring the water down to a simmer over medium-low heat. Cover with a lid, and reduce the heat to low. Once the rice has absorbed the water, remove from the heat and set aside.

Mix the rice vinegar, sugar, and salt in a small saucepan over medium heat. Once the sugar dissolves, add this solution to the rice. Stir well and cover with a clean dish towel. Once cooled, separate the rice into two bowls. Stir the sesame seeds into one bowl of rice.

Place a seaweed sheet on the sushi mat, bright-side down. Then, using the back of a spoon, spread a layer of rice evenly on the seaweed sheet, leaving about a 1/4-inch border on the edges with no rice.

Lay some of the vegetable and fish strips over the rice, lengthwise. A standard roll includes one strip each of cucumber, carrot, and fish, topped with avocado. But, of course, you can make them however you want! Don't be afraid to try different things! Once you've topped the seaweed and rice, you're ready to roll.

Dip your fingertips in a little bit of water, and spread it on the border of the seaweed sheet, where there's no rice. Roll the mat forward, making sure you press the rice, vegetables, and fish between your fingers, rolling everything together tightly. Keep rolling the sushi roll, back and forth, and when you finish, squeeze the sushi mat for a few seconds. Double check that the ends of the seaweed sheet stick to each other, as this is what will hold the roll together.

Once the roll is rolled firmly, dip a very sharp knife in water, and then carefully slice the roll into bite-size pieces. Try to make the pieces of equal size, and dip your knife in water after each cut.

When all of your rolls are ready, place them on a serving plate alongside pickled ginger, soy sauce, and wasabi paste. It's ready and delicious!

If you have any leftover fish or rice, you can make nigiri. Make small balls of rice by squeezing them firmly, and then place a piece of fish on top.

GRILLED FISH WITH CHIMICHURRI SAUCE

BY CHARLOTTE WHEATON

" This recipe is really easy, and it is best served hot from the pan. At first glance, the sauce may seem a little overpowering, but it is actually a nice counterpoint to the fish. "

 20 MINS : SERVES 4

INGREDIENTS

For the Chimichurri Sauce

1 cup fresh leafy herbs, such as basil, parsley, and cilantro, chopped (seasonal)

Juice of 1 lemon

2 garlic cloves

½ teaspoon red pepper flakes

⅓ cup extra-virgin olive oil

Salt and pepper

For the Fish

2 tablespoons extra-virgin olive oil

4 white fish fillets, such as halibut, striped bass, or cod (about 6 ounces each; see Quick Tip)

Salt and pepper

To make the chimichurri sauce: Combine the herbs, lemon juice, garlic, and red pepper flakes in a food processor. Pulse while slowly incorporating the olive oil. Pulse until combined. Taste and season with salt and pepper.

To make the fish: Generously season both sides of the fish fillets with salt and pepper.

Heat the oil in a large frying pan over medium-high heat. When the oil is almost smoking, about 1 minute, add the fish and cook until opaque throughout, about 4 minutes per side.

Transfer to a platter and spoon the chimichurri sauce over the fish. Serve immediately.

> **QUICK TIP** The trick to cooking fish on the stovetop is to get your oil very hot before you place the fish in the pan— you should hear it sizzle when you place it in. You will know when to flip the fish, when you see that it is white (opaque) about half way through.

FISH CURRY WITH SPICED RICE

BY SALIM VIJRI

"This dish is a personal favorite for its simplicity but real depth of flavor, if the spices are balanced right. Being half Indian, I was brought up with this kind of fresh and aromatic cooking!"

45 MINS : SERVES 2–3

INGREDIENTS

For the Spiced Rice

1 tablespoon extra-virgin olive oil

1 teaspoon whole fennel seeds

1 teaspoon turmeric

¾ cup basmati rice

For the Curry

1 pound cod fish fillet, cut into 2 to 3 pieces

1 to 2 tablespoons curry paste

1 tablespoon extra-virgin olive oil

½ teaspoon ground fennel seeds

½ teaspoon ground coriander

½ teaspoon garam masala

2 green onions, chopped

1 red onion, chopped

1 garlic clove, minced

1 (15-ounce) can coconut milk

1 teaspoon fresh cilantro, chopped

½ teaspoon chili powder

1 tablespoon fresh lemon or lime juice

Salt and pepper

¼ cup chopped pistachio nuts

To make the spiced rice: Bring a kettle of water to a boil. Heat the olive oil in a medium saucepan over medium heat. Add the fennel seeds and turmeric and cook, stirring, until fragrant. Add the rice and stir until glistening with oil. Add boiling water to

just cover the rice. Cover the pan and cook for 6 to 7 minutes. Remove from heat and stir with a fork.

To make the curry: Rub both sides of the fish with some of the curry paste, saving the rest for later. Heat the olive oil in a large frying pan over medium-high heat. Add the ground fennel, ground coriander, and garam masala and cook, stirring, until fragrant. Add the fish and cook for 10 minutes, turning it over now and then to avoid burning.

Increase the heat to medium-high and add the green onions, red onion, and garlic. Sauté the onions until softened. Add the remaining curry paste, coconut milk, cilantro, and chili powder. Cook for a few minutes, until the fish starts to flake apart. Add the citrus juice, and season with salt and pepper. Transfer to a serving platter and sprinkle with pistachio nuts.

ROASTED SALMON WITH HOLLANDAISE SAUCE

BY LOLA DE COURROUX

"To me, this is real cooking. You've got four elements here that complement each other: The lemon is going to bring together the fish and the sauce and the garlic will make the spinach and the potatoes sing. Happy eating!"

55 MINS : SERVES 4

INGREDIENTS

For the Salmon
1 tablespoon extra-virgin olive oil

20 to 25 new potatoes

6 garlic cloves, minced

2 tablespoons fresh thyme, chopped

Salt and pepper

4 (6-ounce) salmon fillets

1 lemon, quartered

2 tablespoons dried dillweed

1 tablespoon butter

2 cups fresh spinach leaves

For the Hollandaise Sauce
2 large egg yolks

Salt and pepper

1 tablespoon butter

1 to 2 tablespoons white wine vinegar

Juice of ½ lemon

To make the salmon: Place one oven rack in the upper third of the oven, and another near the middle. Preheat the oven to 350°F. Coat a roasting pan with the oil, and leave in the oven to heat.

Bring a large pot of water to a boil and boil the potatoes for 15 minutes. Drain, transfer to a large bowl, and toss with the garlic and thyme. Season with salt and pepper. Set aside.

Place each salmon fillet in the middle of a square of parchment paper. Squeeze a lemon quarter over each fillet. Sprinkle with the dill and season with salt and pepper. Wrap the fillets in foil and place them side by side on a baking dish.

Take the hot roasting pan out of the oven. Add the potatoes and roll them around in the oil. Place on the top rack of the oven. Put the baking dish with the salmon in the oven as well, on the middle rack. Everything will take about 20 minutes to cook. After 10 minutes, roll the potatoes around in the pan again so they cook evenly.

Melt the butter with the remaining garlic in a medium frying pan. Add the spinach and stir until it wilts. Decrease the heat to low.

To make the sauce: Put the egg yolks in a mixing bowl and season with salt and pepper. Whisk vigorously for about 1 minute.

Melt the butter in a small saucepan or in the microwave. Heat the vinegar and lemon juice in another small saucepan over medium heat until they start to foam. Add the egg yolks while whisking vigorously. Slowly add the butter, and whisk for another 30 seconds. Remove from the heat.

Pour the sauce over the fish and serve with the potatoes.

HONEY PRAWNS WITH CHILE AND ROSEMARY

BY EDWARD GOSLING

"It's really easy to change the quantities in this recipe, depending on how many people you're cooking for. Once you've cooked it a couple of times, throw out all my measurements and just add according to what you like – a big glug of oil, a generous pour of honey . . ."

25 MINS : SERVES 4

INGREDIENTS

24 large raw prawns (shrimp), shelled and deveined

4 cloves garlic, minced, plus more for garnish

1 large jalapeño chile, seeded and finely chopped, plus more for garnish

4 to 5 sprigs rosemary, chopped, plus more for garnish

Salt and pepper

6 tablespoons honey (good-quality lavender or orange blossom), plus more for drizzling

¼ cup extra-virgin olive oil (a really good one), plus more for drizzling

1 baguette, sliced

1 (8-ounce) bag of seasonal greens (spinach, arugula, or watercress, for example)

1 avocado (optional)

1 lemon (optional)

Put the prawns in a mixing bowl with the garlic, jalapeño (make sure you remove the seeds first—you want the heat and flavor of the chile, not something that will blow your head off!), and rosemary. Season with salt and pepper. Add the honey and olive oil and stir.

Heat a wok over high heat and add the prawn mixture. Watch it sizzle, bubble, and get tasty. Once the prawns turn pink on the outside and opaque on the inside (about 5 minutes), remove from the heat.

Put two slices of bread on each plate. Pile the seasonal greens in the center of the plate. Top with sliced avocado, if you like. Add an equal amount of cooked shrimp to each plate. Drizzle the greens with honey and sprinkle with lemon and sauce from the wok.

SIZZLING STEAK WITH MASHED POTATOES

BY ALAINE LEMAIRE

"No one turns down a steak. A lot of young people think that steak is difficult to cook, but I wanted to show that it is a simple thing to make but still delicious."

40 MINS : SERVES 4

INGREDIENTS

4 rib-eye steaks

2 tablespoons malt vinegar

Salt and pepper

2 pounds Yukon gold potatoes, peeled and halved

2 tablespoons butter

½ cup heavy cream

Salt and pepper

2 cups frozen peas

2 tablespoons sunflower oil

Drizzle the steaks with the vinegar and season with salt and pepper. Cover with plastic wrap and put in the fridge.

Bring a large pot of salted water to a boil and add the potatoes. Boil until soft, about 20 minutes. Drain the water and mash the potatoes in the pot. Put back over low heat, stirring constantly. Mix in the butter and heavy cream. Season with salt and pepper. Remove from the heat and cover to keep warm.

Add enough water to cover the peas in a small saucepan. Bring to a boil and add the frozen peas. Cook for 5 minutes, and then drain. Meanwhile, heat a large frying pan over high heat. When it starts to smoke, lower the heat and add the sunflower oil. Fry the steaks for 1 minute on each side for a rare steak (a little longer if you like your steak well done).

Serve the steaks with the mashed potatoes and peas, pouring the juice from the steak over the dish.

LEMON–TARRAGON CHICKEN

BY JACK VEJVODA

"This is a super-easy family meal to prepare when you want to impress people with your culinary skills. (It's pretty hard to mess up.)"

 1.5 HRS : SERVES 4

INGREDIENTS

One 4- to 5-pound whole chicken
2 lemons, halved
Salt and pepper
2 teaspoons dried tarragon
2 sprigs fresh tarragon

Preheat the oven to 450°F.

Remove any giblets from the chicken, trim the excess fat, and rinse and pat dry. Place the chicken, breast-side up, in a shallow roasting pan. Squeeze the lemons over the chicken and sprinkle with salt, pepper, and dried tarragon. Place 2 of the squeezed lemon halves and the tarragon sprigs in the cavity of the chicken.

Place on a rack in the middle of the oven. Roast for 20 minutes. Reduce the oven to 375°F and continue roasting, basting 2 or 3 times with the pan juices, until the chicken is golden brown and a meat thermometer inserted into the thickest part of the thigh registers 165°F, about 1 hour.

Let the chicken rest for at least 10 minutes to allow its juices to settle before carving.

QUICK TIPS   Using a meat thermometer can be tricky. You need to carefully stick the meat thermometer into the thickest part of the thigh, without touching the bone. You will also know when the chicken is done if the juices run clear when pricked with a fork and the drumstick moves easily in its socket (wiggle it to check!). ※ Chicken cooks at about 20 minutes per pound, so you can use this recipe for any size bird by adjusting the cooking time (just make sure the meat thermometer reads 165°F before you take it out of the oven). ※ You can toss quartered potatoes and chopped carrots in the pan to cook alongside the chicken if you want to cook an entire meal at once.

CHICKEN–CHORIZO CASSEROLE

BY CHARLES PATTERSON

"This is a good meal to cook when you have friends around, because it's easy to make huge quantities of it, and it usually pleases everyone. A good Saturday night meal."

2.5 HRS : SERVES 6

INGREDIENTS

For the Roasted Tomatoes

5 large tomatoes, halved

5 garlic cloves, halved

1 tablespoon extra-virgin olive oil

2 teaspoons fresh thyme, chopped

Salt and pepper

For the Roasted New Potatoes

2 pounds new potatoes

3 garlic cloves, minced

2 tablespoons vegetable oil

1 to 2 teaspoons fresh thyme leaves

Salt and pepper

For the Casserole

2 teaspoons extra-virgin olive oil

4 garlic cloves, minced

½ cup fresh basil, chopped

1 onion, diced

4 boneless, skinless chicken breasts, chopped into 1-inch cubes

2 Spanish chorizo sausages, chopped

2 red bell peppers, chopped

1 yellow bell pepper, chopped

1 (28-ounce) can chopped tomatoes

¼ cup white wine

Salt and pepper

To make the roasted tomatoes: Preheat the oven to 375°F. Place the tomatoes, cut-side up, in a large roasting pan. Top each tomato half with a garlic half. Drizzle with olive oil and season with thyme, salt, and pepper. Roast for 30 to 40 minutes, or until lightly charred.

To make the roasted new potatoes: Boil the potatoes for 5 minutes (they should be soft, but not cooked through). Drain and put on a roasting pan. Toss with the garlic, vegetable oil, thyme, salt, and pepper. Roast for 30 to 40 minutes, or until you can easily pierce through them with a fork.

To make the casserole: Heat the oil in a large frying pan over medium heat and add the garlic and basil; cook until fragrant, about 2 to 3 minutes. Add the onion, and cook until golden brown. Add the chicken and cook, stirring, for 5 minutes. Add the chorizo and the red and yellow bell peppers and cook for 1 to 2 minutes. Add the tomatoes and wine. Season with salt and pepper. Simmer, stirring occasionally, for 30 minutes, or until the sauce is reduced and thickened.

VEGETARIAN GREEN CHILE ENCHILADAS

BY CAMERON KING

"If you don't need to feed a bunch of people, you can easily use a smaller baking dish and use a bit less of everything – just fit in as many enchiladas as you can and cover with sauce and cheese. Then serve with chips and salsa. Pretty easy!"

1.25 HRS · SERVES 10

INGREDIENTS

20 corn tortillas (6 inches in diameter)

2 (16-ounce) cans vegetarian refried beans (see Quick Tips)

½ cup salsa (see Quick Tips)

6 ounces button mushrooms, thickly sliced

3 small zucchini, chopped

½ onion, chopped

3 (10-ounce) cans green chile sauce

5 cups shredded Monterey Jack cheese

Sour cream for garnish (optional)

> **QUICK TIPS**   You can use homemade beans if you prefer; see page 30. ❋ You can make homemade salsa if you prefer; see page 33. ❋ You can make this dish a day or two ahead. Just cover the assembled enchiladas with plastic wrap and store in the refrigerator until you are ready to bake it. ❋ If you prefer a meaty version, add ground beef or cooked chicken and use fewer veggies. ❋ This dish can be made in any season: use shredded brussels sprouts instead of the zucchini for winter or chopped kale for a hearty fall dish.

Preheat the oven to 350°F.

Fill a vegetable steamer with a couple of inches of water and bring to a boil. Using tongs, place one tortilla at a time in the steamer and heat until pliable but not sticky, about 30 seconds. Place the steamed tortillas on a plate and set aside.

Heat the beans in a saucepan over low heat. Stir in the salsa and continue stirring until just heated. Transfer to a bowl. Line up the beans and the remaining ingredients, except the sour cream, in preparation for assembling the enchiladas.

Set a tortilla on a work surface. Place 2 tablespoons of beans in the center of the tortilla, top with 1 tablespoon each of mushrooms and zucchini (about 4 pieces of each), ½ teaspoon onion, and a heaping 2 tablespoons of cheese. Roll up and place seam-side down in a 15-by-10-inch baking dish. Repeat with the remaining tortillas and filling, creating rows, until all the enchiladas have been assembled and placed in the dish.

Cover with green chile sauce and sprinkle generously with cheese. Bake for 45 minutes, or until hot and bubbly. Let cool slightly and serve with sour cream, if desired.

SEASONAL LASAGNA

Lasagna is truly an evergreen dish. A rich, tomato-based lasagna is great in the winter when you need rib-sticking comfort food to warm up and feel cozy. It's also great during the warmer months, cooked with light cheese and seasonally fresh veggies. Play around and swap out the ingredients in this recipe for whatever looks good at your local farmers' market.

SERVES 6-8

SUMMER LASAGNA

2 HRS

INGREDIENTS

12 dried lasagna noodles

3 tablespoons extra-virgin olive oil

1 medium red onion, chopped

4 garlic cloves, minced

2 pounds summer squash or zucchini, cut into half-moons

3 cups mixed mushrooms, like cremini or oyster, chopped

½ teaspoon red pepper flakes

2 tablespoons tomato paste

1 (28-ounce) can chopped tomatoes, with their juice

1 (15-ounce) can tomato purée

½ cup vegetable stock

1 pound fresh ricotta

2½ cups whole-milk mozzarella

½ cup grated Parmesan cheese

¼ cup fresh parsley, chopped

⅓ cup fresh basil, chopped

Salt and pepper

1 large egg, beaten

Preheat the oven to 375°F. Bring a large pot of salted water to a boil and cook the noodles according to the package directions. Drain and rinse in cold water. Set aside to dry on paper towels in a single layer.

Heat the olive oil in a large saucepan or a pot over medium heat. Add the onion and garlic, and cook for about 5 minutes. Add the squash, mushrooms, and red pepper flakes. Cook, stirring occasionally, until softened, about 10 minutes. Add the tomato paste and stir well, so everything is coated. Add the chopped tomatoes and their juice, stir, and cook for about 5 minutes. Add the tomato purée and vegetable stock. Bring to a boil, lower the heat, and simmer until the sauce thickens, about 15 minutes.

Meanwhile, mix the ricotta, mozzarella, and Parmesan cheeses in a medium bowl. Stir in the parsley and basil, and season with salt and pepper. Fold in the egg.

Put one ladle full of the vegetable sauce in the bottom of a 9-by-13-inch baking dish, spreading it evenly. Top with 4 lasagna noodles. Spread some of the cheese mixture on the top of the noodles, top with 2 ladles full of sauce, and then 4 more lasagna noodles. Repeat the layers until all the noodles are used, ending with the noodles. Top with 2 more ladles of vegetable sauce and a few dollops of the remaining cheese.

Bake for about 25 minutes, or until the noodles are cooked through and the cheese and sauce are bubbling. Let rest for about 15 minutes before serving.

> **QUICK TIP** Use a slotted spoon to transfer the vegetable sauce to the lasagna. This way, the layer will be mostly the chopped tomatoes and vegetables, and you can spoon on the liquid sauce separately, depending on how much you want to add. Be careful not to add too much liquid; nobody likes a soggy lasagna!

WINTER LASAGNA

3.5 HRS

INGREDIENTS

¼ cup extra-virgin olive oil

1 pound ground beef

8 mild Italian sausages (about 1½ pounds), casings removed

5 garlic cloves, minced

½ teaspoon red pepper flakes

3 tablespoons tomato paste

1 (28-ounce) can chopped tomatoes, with their juice

1 (28-ounce) can tomato purée

1 cup chicken or beef stock (see page 34)

1 bay leaf

1 tablespoon fresh thyme leaves

1 teaspoon sugar

12 dried lasagna noodles (see Quick Tips)

1½ pounds fresh ricotta

2 cups shredded whole-milk mozzarella

½ cup fresh basil, chopped

1 large egg, beaten

Grated Parmesan cheese for sprinkling

Heat the olive oil in a large pot over medium-high heat. Add the ground beef and sausage and cook, breaking up the sausage, until cooked through. Add the garlic and red pepper flakes. Add the tomato paste, stirring until well incorporated. Add the tomatoes and their juice, the tomato purée, stock, bay leaf, thyme, and sugar. Bring to a boil, lower the heat, and simmer for at least 1½ hours.

Preheat the oven to 375°F. Bring a large pot of salted water to a boil and cook the noodles according to the package directions. Drain and rinse in cold water. Set aside to dry on paper towels in a single layer.

Meanwhile, mix the ricotta, mozzarella, basil, and egg in a medium bowl; season with salt and pepper.

Put one ladle full of the meat sauce in the bottom of a 9-by-13-inch baking dish, spreading it evenly. Top with 4 lasagna noodles. Spread some of the cheese mixture on the top of the noodles, top with 2 ladles of sauce, and then 4 more lasagna noodles. Repeat layering until all the noodles are used, ending with the noodles. Top with 2 ladles full of meat sauce and sprinkle with the Parmesan cheese.

Bake for about 40 minutes, or until the noodles are cooked through and the cheese and sauce are bubbling. Let rest for about 15 minutes before serving.

> **QUICK TIPS** Instead of boiling dried lasagna noodles, look for "no-boil" lasagna noodles in grocery stores. They're ready to put right in the baking dish, no boiling necessary. These noodles bake nicely and save time and work. ※ Lasagna keeps great in the freezer. If you're not serving a large crowd, wrap and store half of the lasagna in the freezer. To reheat, thaw and then bake in a 325°F oven for about 25 minutes.

DESSERTS

ALMOND CAKE OR PAIN DE GÊNES

BY LAURANE MARCHIVE

"This is a cake my mother used to make a lot. And I think it's my favorite ever. It seems almost impossible to mess it up, and it's just delicious. Maybe not the healthiest cake ever but, hey, we all need to indulge a bit from time to time."

1.25 HRS : MAKES 1 CAKE

INGREDIENTS

½ cup (1 stick) unsalted butter, plus more for the pan
½ cup whole almonds, with brown skins on
⅔ cup sugar
3 large eggs
3 tablespoons all-purpose flour
2 tablespoons rum
¼ teaspoon salt

Preheat the oven to 300°F. Line the bottom of a standard-size cake pan with parchment paper and smear the paper and the sides of the pan with butter.

In a blender or food processor, grind the almonds with half of the sugar.

In a large bowl, use a fork to beat the butter and remaining sugar together until creamy. Stir in the ground almonds. Add the eggs, one by one, stirring vigorously after each addition. Once the eggs are well incorporated, stir in the flour, rum, and salt.

Pour the batter into the cake pan and bake for 40 to 50 minutes, or until a toothpick stuck into the center of the cake comes out clean. Let cool in the pan for 10 minutes. Remove from the pan and let cool completely on a rack.

PEAR AND ALMOND TART

BY DOMINIC MCINNES

"Baking is a great way to bring people together. There's nothing better than sharing a good cake with friends."

40 MINS : MAKES 1 TART

INGREDIENTS

⅓ cup all-purpose flour

¾ cup powdered sugar

⅔ cup ground almonds

5 large egg whites

¾ cup plus 2 tablespoons (1¾ sticks) unsalted butter, melted

3 pears, peeled and sliced lengthwise

⅓ cup sliced almonds

Preheat the oven to 375°F.

Sift the flour and powdered sugar into a large bowl. Stir in the ground almonds.

Whisk the egg whites in another large bowl until frothy. Add the butter, stirring until well incorporated. Pour into a baking dish. Top with the sliced pears and sliced almonds.

Bake for about 25 minutes, or until the base is firm. Eat!

QUICK TIPS   To separate the egg whites from the yolk, pass the raw egg back and forth from one half of the shell to the other so the white drips into a bowl and the yolk remains in the shell. You can reserve the yolks to make homemade mayonnaise (see page 33). ✳ To enjoy this tart in any season, replace the pears with whatever fruit looks great at your local farmers' market: plums and apricots in the spring, mixed berries in the summer, apples in the fall, or figs in the winter.

OATMEAL COOKIES

BY JACK LOWE

"Excellent cookies and super-simple to make!"

 40 MINS : MAKES 18 COOKIES

INGREDIENTS

½ cup self-rising flour

⅓ cup old-fashioned rolled oats (not instant)

¼ cup brown sugar

¼ cup raisins

6½ tablespoons margarine, softened

3 tablespoons maple syrup

½ teaspoon ground cinnamon

½ teaspoon ground nutmeg

Preheat the oven to 350°F. Grease a baking sheet.

Mix the flour and oats in a large mixing bowl. Stir in the sugar and raisins. Add the margarine and continue to mix until well incorporated. Fold in the syrup, cinnamon, and nutmeg.

Form the dough into eighteen equal balls. Flatten the balls and place on the baking sheet. Bake for 15 to 20 minutes, or until lightly browned. Let cool for 10 to 15 minutes.

MINIATURE CHOCOLATE COOKIES

BY AMELIA WELLS

"These cookies may not solve all the world's problems, but if you make them vegan, that's at least a good start."

30 MINS : MAKES 15–18 COOKIES

INGREDIENTS

6 ounces dark chocolate

½ cup brown sugar

2 ounces unsalted butter (use Vitalite or another dairy-free spread for vegan cookies)

1¾ cups all-purpose flour

½ teaspoon baking powder

Preheat the oven to 325°F.

Melt 5 ounces of the chocolate and set aside. Grate the remaining ounce.

Beat the sugar and butter together in a large mixing bowl. Add the melted chocolate and stir to incorporate. Stir in the flour and baking powder.

Roll the cookie dough into 15 to 18 balls and transfer to a baking sheet. Flatten the cookies and top with grated chocolate. Bake for 10 to 12 minutes.

They're ready!

CRÈME BRÛLÉE

BY MARIUS CAREY

"Well, since I was a kid I've loved playing with fire, and I've always had a passion for cooking, so mix the two, and you get the best of both, crème brûlée."

2.5 HRS : SERVES 6

INGREDIENTS

½ cup lavender sugar (see Quick Tips)
6 large egg yolks
1 teaspoon vanilla extract (see Quick Tips)
2 cups heavy cream
Sugar for sprinkling
Fresh berries, such as strawberries, blueberries, or raspberries for serving (seasonal)

Preheat the oven to 325°F.

In a medium bowl, whisk together the lavender sugar, egg yolks, and vanilla extract until well blended.

In a thick-bottomed saucepan over medium heat, scald the cream until small bubbles begin to form along the edges of the pan (do not boil); it will register about 180°F on a kitchen thermometer (see Quick Tips). Very slowly and carefully, whisk the hot cream into the egg yolk mixture, and continue whisking until fully combined.

Pour the custard into four 6-ounce ramekins until about three-quarters full and set them in a deep roasting pan. Carefully pour hot water into the roasting pan until it reaches about half way up the ramekins. Place in the oven, on the middle or lower rack, and bake until set (they should jiggle slightly in the middle when shaken), about 20 to 25 minutes. Remove from the oven and let cool for about

15 minutes. Chill until firm, 30 minutes to 2 hours (depending on whether you want to serve them warm or cold).

Sprinkle the chilled brûlées with the sugar. Using a kitchen torch (see Quick Tips), caramelize the sugar by moving the flame constantly over the surface in a slow, circular motion until browned and caramelized (you'll know you are close enough when the sugar starts to liquefy). Garnish with fresh berries and serve.

QUICK TIPS You can find lavender sugar in specialty stores or online. ✳ You can substitute almond extract for the vanilla if that sounds good. ✳ Crème brûlée literally means "scorched cream." Although cream is now pasteurized and does not have to be heated to kill bacteria, heating it improves the density and texture of custards. If you don't have a kitchen thermometer, just heat until you see bubbles around the edges. ✳ Read the manufacturer's instructions for the kitchen torch before you use it—you should know how to remove the safety and turn it on and off before you fire it up. Adjust the flame to medium and be sure to remove any flammable items, such as dish towels, from your work surface.

TAPIOCA PUDDING

BY SARAH EISENFISZ

"I love this dessert because it reminds me of my childhood. When I was little, my mom often made it for me, and now it's really cool to make it for other people. It doesn't require too many ingredients, which is always a good thing when you feel too lazy to go to the store."

20 MINS : SERVES 4–6

INGREDIENTS

3 cups milk

⅓ cup pearl tapioca

⅓ cup sugar

½ teaspoon extract (vanilla, orange blossom, almond, cacao, or coconut)

¼ teaspoon sea salt

Put all of the ingredients in a medium saucepan over medium heat. Bring to a boil while stirring with a wooden spoon. As the sauce thickens, tapioca pearls will gradually form.

Once the milk is completely absorbed, pour into individual ramekins. This is delicious served either warm or cold.

QUICK TIP If chilling before serving, put the pudding (after it cools) in a bowl and tightly cover with plastic wrap, pressing it lightly against the surface. This will keep the pudding moist and prevent a "skin" from forming on top.

CARROT CAKE

BY PIA HIMMELSTERN

"I like this carrot cake recipe because even though people might raise their eyebrows at first, in the end, everyone loves it!"

1 HR : MAKES 1 CAKE

INGREDIENTS

3 carrots
4 large eggs
1 cup vegetable oil
2 cups sugar
1 cup all-purpose flour
1 teaspoon baking powder

Preheat the oven to 375°F.

Boil the carrots in a saucepan of water for 15 minutes. Cool under cold running water and grate.

Mix the carrots, eggs, and oil in a large bowl. Add the sugar and the baking powder and flour. Mix together until smooth.

Pour into a cake pan . Bake for about 30 minutes, or until a cake tester inserted in the middle comes out clean. Let cool and enjoy!

ROSE PETAL SWEETS

BY CAMILLE LELOIRE

"These sweets are really easy to make and they can be a perfect snack! I love them because they're so unusual – I guess we're not used to eating flowers that much! It's actually a really good recipe if you have a garden or homegrown roses, as you wouldn't want to eat the pesticides on industrial flowers."

2.5 HRS : MAKES 2 SNACK-SIZED SERVINGS

INGREDIENTS

1 large egg white
3 to 5 tablespoons powdered sugar
Petals of 3 organic roses, washed with cold water

Combine the egg white in a medium bowl with enough of the powdered sugar so the mixture is slightly sticky. Mix well.

One by one, dip the petals in the egg white mixture and lay on parchment paper. Sprinkle half of the remaining sugar over the rose petals. Let dry for 1 to 2 hours. Flip the petals, and sprinkle with the remaining sugar.

One the petals have dried completely, they are ready to eat! Keep them dry. Eat as a snack or use them to decorate cakes. They look brilliant. *Bon appétit!*

APPLE CHIPS

BY LAURENT QUINTAL

"This is a really good treat and easy to make, especially when you have apples sitting somewhere in a cabinet getting old. Just stick them in the oven and you can make delicious chips."

 2.5 HRS : SERVES 4–6

INGREDIENTS

5 apples, peeled and thinly sliced

¼ cup brown sugar

1 tablespoon spice, such as ground cinnamon or nutmeg, single or mixed

Heat the oven to 325°F.

Arrange the apple slices on a baking sheet. Sprinkle the sugar and spice on the apples. Bake for 2 hours, flipping them over halfway through.

Store the apple chips for a few days in a dry place.

QUICK TIP   You can use just about any apple variety for this recipe, but the crisper and tastier the apple, the better. Think Gala, Granny Smith, Honeycrisp, and Golden Delicious.

CHEESECAKE

BY ELLA VEJVODA

"I like to cook with my mom on the weekends. My favorite thing is to make desserts. Chocolate chip cookies and cheesecake are my specialties!"

7 HRS : MAKES 1 CAKE

INGREDIENTS

1¾ cups graham cracker crumbs (see Quick Tips)

4 tablespoons unsalted butter, melted

1⅓ cups sugar

1 tablespoon all-purpose flour

4 (8-ounce) packages cream cheese, softened

Zest of 1 lemon (see Quick Tips)

1 teaspoon vanilla extract

¼ cup heavy cream

1 large egg yolk plus 3 whole eggs

Fresh berries, such as strawberries, raspberries, or blueberries for serving (seasonal)

Preheat the oven to 325°F. Grease a 9-inch springform pan.

Mix the graham cracker crumbs and melted butter together in a small bowl. Pour this mixture into the pan, and press evenly against the bottom of the pan.

In another small bowl, mix together the sugar and flour, and set aside.

Using an electric mixer, beat the cream cheese until smooth in a large bowl. Continue to beat the cream cheese while slowly adding in the sugar mixture. Add the lemon zest, vanilla, and heavy cream while continuing to mix. Add the egg yolk and whole eggs, one at a time. Beat until smooth.

Pour the batter over the graham crackers. Place the pan in the oven and cook until the cake is set (it should not be too jiggly), about 60 to 70 minutes. Remove from the oven and let cool. Chill for at least 5 hours and remove the sides from the springform pan before serving.

Garnish with fresh berries and serve.

> QUICK TIPS   This cheesecake has to chill for at least 5 hours or overnight to give it time to set, so make sure you plan accordingly! ✳ You can buy graham cracker crumbs or put whole graham crackers in a resealable plastic bag and roll a rolling pin over them. ✳ Zest is basically grated citrus peel. To make orange zest, grate the fruit as you would cheese, just make sure to use the smallest holes on your grater. You can also use a zester, which will create fine, long strips, which you can then mince.

CREPES WITH ORANGE SAUCE

BY JULES ALLAIRE

"My dad taught me how to flip crepes right in the pan when I was very young. Our family celebrates Chandeleur, or Crepe Day, where you flip crepes with a coin in your hand, and if the crepe lands in the pan, you will be prosperous all year."

30 MIN : MAKES 8 CREPES

INGREDIENTS

For the Orange Sauce

½ cup (1 stick) unsalted butter, at room temperature

½ cup sugar

Zest of 2 oranges (see Quick Tips, page 122)

1¼ cups fresh squeezed orange juice

For the Crepes

1 cup all-purpose flour

¼ teaspoon salt

2 eggs

1½ cups milk

2 tablespoons butter, melted, plus more for pan

3 oranges, segmented, for serving (optional; see Quick Tips)

To make the orange sauce: Heat a small saucepan over medium heat. Add the butter, sugar, and orange zest. When the butter melts and sugar dissolves, add the orange juice. Bring to a boil and cook until the volume of liquid has reduced by half and becomes the consistency of syrup, about 5 to 10 minutes. Set aside.

To make the crepes: In a small bowl, sift together the flour and salt, and set aside. In a large bowl, using a whisk, beat the eggs until the whites and yolks are incorporated. Add the milk and butter, and beat until smooth. Stir in the flour mixture one-quarter at a time and beat until smooth. The batter should be thin, but have the consistency of heavy cream. If the batter is too thick, add more milk, stirring in a little at a time. If the batter is too thin, add more flour, a tablespoon at a time.

Heat a medium frying pan over medium-high heat. Once hot, melt ½ teaspoon of butter in the pan. Ladle ¼ cup of batter into the pan and tilt the pan in a circular motion until the bottom is covered with batter. Cook the crepe for 30 to 50 seconds, or until it is slightly moist on top and the edges are beginning to brown.

Loosen the edges of the crepe, slide the spatula under it, and then gently flip it. Cook for 30 seconds more and transfer to a plate (see Quick Tips). Repeat the process with the remaining batter.

To serve, fold the crepes in half and then fold in half again, forming wedge shapes. Drizzle with orange sauce and serve with orange slices, if desired.

> **QUICK TIPS** Your first crepe will most likely not to be perfect, but don't worry, you will get the hang of it—just the right amount of heat, butter, and batter—soon enough. ✳ You can place a layer of parchment paper between each crepe to keep them from sticking together while you are waiting to serve them. ✳ Oranges are available year-round, but you can make sauce for the crepes (or fill the crepes) with any seasonal fruit that strikes your fancy. You can also make savory crepes, filled with cheese, ham, cooked chicken, and sautéed veggies of your choice.

OREO CUPCAKES

BY DANIELLE BURNS

"This is the perfect dessert to make for parties or for when you just feel like baking."

50 MINS : MAKES 12 CUPCAKES

INGREDIENTS

For the Cupcakes

12 Oreos

1½ cups all-purpose flour

1 cup sugar

1½ teaspoons baking powder

½ teaspoon salt

7 tablespoons unsalted butter, softened

½ cup sour cream

1 large egg plus 2 large egg yolks

1 teaspoon vanilla extract

For the Frosting

½ cup (1 stick) unsalted butter, softened

¼ cup cocoa powder

2 cups powdered sugar

1 teaspoon vanilla extract

½ teaspoon salt

1 tablespoon sour cream

10 Oreo cookies, crushed

Preheat the oven to 350°F.

Fill a 12-cup cupcake tin with paper liners. Put an Oreo cookie at the bottom of each liner.

To make the cupcakes: In a large bowl, whisk together the flour, sugar, baking powder, and salt. In another bowl, beat the butter, sour cream, egg, egg yolks, and vanilla until smooth. Fold the wet ingredients into the dry ingredients until incorporated. Fill each muffin cup about three-quarters full of batter. Bake for 20 to 25 minutes, or until a cake tester inserted in the middle comes out clean. Let cool before frosting.

To make the frosting: In a large bowl, beat the butter and cocoa powder until smooth. Add the sugar, vanilla, and salt, and continue to beat. Stir in the sour cream.

Frost the cupcakes and top with crushed Oreos.

STRAWBERRY–RHUBARB CRUMBLE

BY EVAN MENDELSON

"This crumble is perfect for dessert or breakfast, but be warned – if you have it for dessert, there probably won't be any left for breakfast! It's that good."

1.25 HRS : SERVES 4

INGREDIENTS

For the Topping

½ cup (1 stick) unsalted butter, softened

¾ cup sugar

¾ cup all-purpose flour

Pinch of ground nutmeg

Pinch of ground cinnamon

For the Filling

4 cups strawberries, hulled and chopped (see Quick Tips)

4 to 6 stalks rhubarb, ends trimmed, and sliced ½ inch thick (see Quick Tips)

Preheat the oven to 350°F.

To make the topping: Combine the butter, sugar, flour, nutmeg, and cinnamon in a food processor. Pulse until the butter is fully incorporated and a smooth, "crumbly" dough is formed, about 1 minute.

To make the filling: In a medium bowl, combine the strawberries and rhubarb. Place the fruit in an 8-by-10-inch baking dish and sprinkle the crumble on top so it covers as much of the surface as possible. Use a Teflon-coated or silicone baking dish to make cleaning easier, or use a ceramic dish for a prettier presentation.

Bake until the topping begins to brown and the fruit is bubbling, about 1 hour.

QUICK TIPS The volume of strawberries and rhubarb should be about equal. However, if you want the crumble to be less tart, use less rhubarb. The exact amount of fruit is not important—you can use as little as 3 cups of each or as many as 8 cups. If you use lots of fruit, the crumble will be more juicy; use less and it will be drier. ✳ Make it your own by adding homemade granola (see page 38) to the crumble just before baking if you like more crunch in the topping. ✳ To make crumble in the fall, substitute apples and pears for the strawberries and rhubarb.

SEASONAL PIES

Everyone loves pie! Especially served with a scoop of ice cream or whipped cream. Make sure to only prepare pies with seasonal fruit and ingredients for the best results.

SERVES 8

FLAKY PIE CRUST

2 HRS

INGREDIENTS

1 cup (2 sticks) cold, unsalted butter

1½ cups all-purpose flour, plus more for dusting

1 teaspoon salt

1½ teaspoons sugar

½ cup ice water

Cut the butter into ½-inch cubes. Return to the refrigerator to keep cold.

Pulse the flour, salt, and sugar in a food processor until blended. Add the butter and pulse (one pulse at a time) until the butter pieces are the size of peas and mixed into the dry ingredients. Add the ice water 1 tablespoon at a time and pulse, until the mixture starts to stick together. You'll know it's ready to go when you squeeze or roll the dough in your hand and it holds together easily. Continue to add water until this consistency is reached. If the dough feels wet or sticky, you've added too much water. If this is the case, add more flour, 1 tablespoon at a time, until the desired consistency is reached.

Empty the dough onto a clean, dry, and lightly floured work surface. Knead briefly so the dough all comes together. (Avoid over-kneading—you should always be able to see bits of butter in the dough.) Break the dough ball into two discs, wrap in plastic wrap, and chill in the refrigerator for at least 1 hour and up to 2 days. Do not skip this step! The chilled butter in the dough is what makes the crust flaky. Meanwhile, while the dough is chilling, prepare a pie filling of your choice.

After the dough is chilled, move one disc to a clean, dry, and lightly floured surface. Use a rolling pin to roll out the dough. Try to keep the shape circular, and roll 11 to 12 inches in diameter. Carefully move the dough into a 9-inch pie tin and trim the edges. Chill in the refrigerator for at least 15 minutes.

Move the pie crust to a work surface and add the pie filling. Roll out the second dough disc into a 10- to 12-inch circle. This will be the top crust of the pie. Either keep it simple and add to the top of the pie as is, cinching the edges closed by pressing with a fork. Cut a few slits into the top so steam can escape while the pie is baking. You could also cut this disc into strips and make a lattice top. Or, use a cookie cutter to cut your favorite shapes from rolled out dough (stars, hearts, anything you like!) and decorate the top of the pie with these dough cut outs. Bake according to specific pie instructions.

SPRING/SUMMER APRICOT AND CHERRY PIE FILLING

50 MINS

INGREDIENTS

1 pound fresh apricots, seeded and quartered
   (leave the skin on)
1½ cups fresh cherries, pitted
⅓ cup sugar
½ teaspoon salt
1 tablespoon fresh lemon juice
⅓ cup all-purpose flour
1 tablespoon unsalted butter, chilled and diced

Preheat the oven to 400°F.

Combine the fresh fruit, sugar, salt, lemon juice, and flour in a large bowl. Stir until the fruit is evenly coated. Evenly fill a pie crust with this filling, and scatter the diced butter on top. Cover with pie crust.

Place on the middle rack in the oven and bake for about 35 to 40 minutes, or until the pie crust is golden brown. Let cool before serving.

FALL/WINTER CLASSIC APPLE PIE FILLING

50 MINS

INGREDIENTS

4 pounds (about 10 to 12) fall apples, such as Granny Smith
   or Gala, peeled, cored, and sliced
⅔ cup sugar, plus 1 tablespoon
2 tablespoons fresh lemon juice
2½ tablespoons all purpose flour
1 tablespoon lemon zest (see Quick Tips, page 122)
½ teaspoon salt
1 teaspoon ground cinnamon
1 teaspoon ground nutmeg
¼ teaspoon ground cloves
1½ tablespoons unsalted butter, chilled and diced
1 egg, beaten

Preheat the oven to 375°F.

In a large bowl, combine the apples, ⅔ cup sugar, lemon juice, flour, lemon zest, salt, and spices. Stir until evenly coated. Taste one apple slice, add more sugar or lemon juice to reach the desired flavor.

Evenly fill a pie crust with the filling. Top the filling with the diced butter, evenly dispersed. Cover with pie crust. Brush the pie top with the egg and sprinkle with the 1 tablespoon of sugar.

Place on the middle rack in the oven and bake for about 55 to 65 minutes, or until the pie crust is golden brown and the apples are bubbling. Let cool before serving.

RESOURCES

FARMERS' MARKETS

These farmers' markets are often rated the best in the US by various national publications. If you happen to live close to one, lucky you! To find a farmers' market near you, check out the USDA National Farmers Market Directory online (www.search.ams.usda.gov/farmersmarkets).

CRESCENT CITY FARMERS' MARKET
NEW ORLEANS, LA
Tuesdays, 9:00 am–1:00 pm, year-round

This markets brings 30+ vendors selling fresh and seasonal produce, meats, and seafood, as well as all kinds of Creole goodies.

DANE COUNTY FARMERS' MARKET
MADISON, WI
Saturdays, 6:00 am–2:00 pm, year-round

Find 200+ local farmers and producers weekly at this market, which dates back to 1972.

DES MOINES FARMERS' MARKET
DES MOINES, IA
Saturdays, 7:00 am–12:00 pm, year-round

This market is one of the best places to get local, sustainably grown and organic food in the Midwest. There are also events for children and live music.

FERRY PLAZA FARMERS' MARKET
SAN FRANCISCO, CA

Saturdays, 8:00 am–2:00 pm, year-round

This market is operated by California's Center for Urban Education and Sustainable Agriculture. Approximately 25,000 people shop at this farmers' market each week.

GREEN CITY MARKET
CHICAGO, IL

Wednesdays and Saturdays, 7:00 am–1:00 pm, year-round

50+ farmers meet here every week to sell organic produce and animal products from animals treated humanely. During the winter, the market moves indoors.

HILO FARMERS' MARKET
HILO, HI

Wednesdays and Saturdays, 6:00 am–4:00 pm

This farmers' market makes the list because of its array of produce unusual to the mainland US, and it's also less touristy than other local markets in Hawaii. There are over 200 vendors here selling all kinds of tropical fruit and vegetables.

NASHVILLE FARMERS' MARKET
NASHVILLE, TN

Daily, 8:00 am–6:00 pm, year-round (enjoy weekly night markets during the summer)

This market can trace its start back to the 1800s! Visitors shop here for their local food and also locally made jewelry, pottery, and crafts.

PORTLAND'S FARMERS' MARKET
PORTLAND, OR

Saturdays, 8:30 am–1:00 pm, March–December

This market is a locavore's dream, with 130+ vendors selling all kinds of strictly regional goods, also including some rare finds, like local yak meat.

SANTA FE FARMERS' MARKET
SANTA FE, NM

Tuesdays (May–November) and Saturdays (year-round), 8:00 am–1:00 pm

This market first started in the 1960s and is now the state's largest farmers' market. The 150+ vendors bring all kinds of edible goods, all produced within Northern New Mexico.

SANTA MONICA FARMERS' MARKET
SANTA MONICA, CA

Wednesdays, 8:30 am– 1:30 pm, year-round

Established in 1981, this is Santa Monica's largest and oldest market.

SFC FARMERS' MARKET
SUNSET VALLEY, TX

Saturdays, 9:00 am–1:00 pm, year-round

This market boasts locally grown and produced food and also includes a huge playground for children.

ST. PAUL FARMERS' MARKET
DOWNTOWN, ST. PAUL, MN

Saturdays, 6:00 am–1:00 pm, May–November

Each of the 167 stalls at this market houses farmers that come from within a 75-mile radius.

UNION SQUARE GREENMARKET
NEW YORK, NY

Mondays, Wednesdays, Fridays, and Saturdays, 8:00 am–6:00 pm, year-round (check for weather-caused closures)

This market started with just a couple of farmers back in 1976, and is now bustling with 140+ local farmers, fishermen, bakers, and artisan food producers. More than 60,000 shoppers visit this market each week.

UNIVERSITY DISTRICT FARMERS' MARKET
SEATTLE, WA

Saturdays, 9:00 am–2:00 pm, year-round

Founded in 1993, this farmers' market boasts 60+ farmers and producers offering produce, dairy, eggs, meats, poultry, seafood, preserves, and baked goods.

COMMUNITY SUPPORTED AGRICULTURE

Through Community Supported Agriculture (CSA), farmers can offer "share boxes" to the public. Usually, for a recurring membership or subscription fee, consumers can purchase a box (or a "share") of seasonal produce, meat, seafood, or eggs—sometimes delivered right to your door. CSAs help farmers run and promote their farms and bring fresh, seasonal, and local food to consumers. Everybody wins! To find your local CSA program, go to localharvest.org/csa.

WHERE TO GO ONLINE

For year-round recipes, food photography, anecdotes, and shopping, check out our favorite food bloggers and websites.

17 AND BAKING
Follow a teen as she chronicles her love of baking.
17andbaking.com

FOOD 52
The newest place to go for food essays, recipes, and to purchase cookware and kitchen supplies.
Food52.com

HAPPY YOLKS
This food blog celebrates wholesome cooking and happy meals.
happyolks.com

THEKITCHN
Apartment Therapy's companion web magazine features kitchen design, cookware, and home cooking.
thekitchn.com

NOT WITHOUT SALT
This blog won the coveted *Saveur*'s Best Cooking Blog in 2013.
notwithoutsalt.com

SMITTEN KITCHEN
This cherished food blog caters to tiny kitchens with little equipment.
smittenkitchen.com

TASTEMADE
There are amazing food and cooking videos on this convenient YouTube channel.
tastemade.com

TASTESPOTTING
This compilation of eye-catching recipes and food photography is culled from the web every day.
tastespotting.com

THUG KITCHEN
This is a fun, vegetarian blog and also noted as *Saveur*'s Best New Food Blog 2013 (warning: explicit language!).
thugkitchen.com

THE YEAR IN FOOD
This blog focuses on seasonal cooking, all year long.
theyearinfood.com

INDEX

EQUIVALENTS

(Some measurements have been rounded.)

LIQUID/DRY MEASUREMENTS

US	METRIC
¼ teaspoon	1.25 milliliters
½ teaspoon	2.5 milliliters
1 teaspoon	5 milliliters
1 tablespoon (3 teaspoons)	15 milliliters
1 fluid ounce (2 tablespoons)	30 milliliters
¼ cup	60 milliliters
⅓ cup	80 milliliters
½ cup	120 milliliters
1 cup	240 milliliters
1 pint (2 cups)	480 milliliters
1 quart (4 cups/32 ounces)	960 milliliters
1 gallon (4 quarts)	3.84 liters
1 ounce (by weight)	28 grams
1 pound	448 grams
2.2 pounds	1 kilogram

OVEN TEMPERATURE

FAHRENHEIT	CELCIUS	GAS
250	120	½
275	140	1
300	150	2
325	160	3
350	180	4
375	190	5
400	200	6
425	220	7
450	230	8
475	240	9
500	260	10

COOKING TERMS

Chopped: Cut into bite-size (or smaller) pieces; chopped food is courser than minced.

Cubed: Cut into cube-shaped pieces ½ inch or larger.

Diced: Cut into dice between ⅛ and to ¼ inch.

Finely diced: Cut into dice less than ½ inch.

Minced: Cut into tiny pieces. Herbs, garlic, and shallots are often minced.

Sliced: Cut into slices ¼- to ½-inch thick.

Thickly sliced: Cut into slices ¾-inch thick or more.

Thinly sliced: Cut into slices less than ¼-inch thick.

CONTRIBUTORS

Laurane Marchive studied journalism at the Institute of Political Sciences, Lille, and Modern French Literature at the Sorbonne, Paris. After working as a journalist in France, Indonesia, and India, she moved to London, where she is now working as an editor, translator, and rights agent. She also works as a freelance circus performer.

Pam McElroy is an editor and caterer living in San Francisco, California, with her husband, Albie, and cat, Stella. She edits books of all genres and caters under the name Meatball Maven. Her favorite hobbies are reading cookbooks cover to cover and cooking epic meals for her friends and family.